GOD

MONTCALM
COMMUNITY COLLEGE
LIBRARY

D1059707

GOD

*Thoughts in an
Age of Uncertainty*

James M. Byrne

New Century Theology

MONTCALM
COMMUNITY COLLEGE
LIBRARY

CONTINUUM
London and New York

Continuum
The Tower Building, 11 York Road, London SE1 7NX
370 Lexington Avenue, New York NY 10017-6503

© 2001 James M. Byrne

All rights reserved. No part of this publication may be reproduced or
transmitted in any form or by any means, electronic or mechanical,
including photocopying, recording or any information storage or
retrieval system, without prior permission in writing from the
publishers.

British Library Cataloguing-in-Publication Data
A catalogue record for this book is available from the British Library.

ISBN: 0-8264-5169-1

29.95

Typeset by Kenneth Burnley, Wirral, Cheshire
Printed and bound in Great Britain by
Biddles Ltd, *www.biddles.co.uk*

Contents

To my family and friends,
for all the conversations

The usual conception of God as one single being outside of the world and behind the world is not the beginning and end of religion. (Friedrich Schleiermacher, *On Religion: Speeches to its Cultured Despisers*, 1988 [1799]).

> Would you model for yourself a pleasant life?
> Worry not about the past
> Let not anger get the upper hand
> Rejoice in the present without ceasing
> Hate no man . . .
> And the future? Abandon it to God.
> (Goethe, *Rule of Life*, quoted in Hadot,
> *Philosophy as a Way of Life*, 1995)

Now faith is the assurance of things hoped for, the conviction of things not seen. (Hebrews 11.1)

For words are wise men's counters, they do but reckon by them; but they are the money of fooles. (Thomas Hobbes, *Leviathan*, 1651)

Introduction

On the wall of my office there is a photograph of a simple mechanical crane hook, suspended in the vertical by a steel wire. The crane (if there is one) is not visible in the photograph and the hook hangs starkly against the backdrop of an open sky, over an open field which rolls away to a woodland with a range of low hills behind. My guess is that the hills are near Louisville, Kentucky, as the photograph was taken by the author, poet, mystic and monk Thomas Merton, who was a member of the community at the nearby Trappist monastery of Gethsemani until his death in December 1968. When I first saw the photograph as a student in the early 1980s it looked to me like an inverted question mark, similar to the upside-down question marks which precede interrogative sentences in written Spanish. The picture of the hook has an eerie, uncertain quality, and perhaps for that reason Merton entitled it 'The Only Known Photograph of God'. The enigmatic photo provided me with a suitable backdrop for writing a book on the impossible. For what, in the end, is God, and how could one possibly attempt to say anything about such an entity? A book on God can only be a failed raid on the intangible and unattainable.

There is only one thing about my subject matter that I know for certain, and that is that I have no idea whether there exists a Being that we can call God. This will seem to many like an inauspicious beginning to a book on the subject, but I would rather think of it as an honest reflection of the true state of our knowledge. I am somewhat consoled in this indeterminate viewpoint by the realization that the Pope, Sigmund Freud, Billy Graham, Karl Marx, Mother Teresa, Bertrand Russell and others who no doubt have, or had, strong views on the subject are not, or were not, in any more privileged position than I am. We can be believers or unbelievers, committed activists in the cause of religion or of secularism, dedicated saints or delirious sinners, but we can never know for certain if there is a God. To put this philosophically, when it comes to God, all of us must be epistemological agnostics. Some might consider this indeterminacy a sad state of affairs, but why should it be so? To me, at least, it is more liberating than carrying the heavy burden of thinking that I know the answer (perhaps this is why so many dedicated believers and unbelievers are so earnest in their certainty).

Of course, if that is all that there is to it, then nothing at all would be said or written on the subject of God, but a great deal is. God is one of those unavoidable topics; almost everyone comes around to it sooner or later. Metaphorically speaking, one way of talking seriously about God is to invite your friends into the room, close the door, and start a discussion within the framework of the things that they and you already consider to be true (for example, that God is three-in-one, that Jesus Christ is the saviour of humanity, or that the true will of God is revealed in the Bible). Within Christian thought, when this internal dialogue is carried on among professional scholars it is commonly known as systematic theology; this is the attempt to explain, delineate, elucidate and explicate 'systematically' the meaning of Christianity from within the context of Christian belief itself. It can be a challenging and rewarding enterprise, and Western civilization would be much impoverished without its presence for most of the past 2,000 years. It is not, however, the approach I am taking in this book.

An alternative metaphor is this: you leave your room and go down to the town square, engage in conversation with whoever you happen to meet there, and see where the discussion leads. This is the more risky option, of course, but it is also potentially more interesting, for you never know what you might hear. You will undoubtedly encounter some strange viewpoints, many of them antagonistic to your own, but you might well learn more than you would by staying in your room with your friends. You might even change your views. There is no formal name for this type of conversation; it is not 'systematic' in the least, although it might be encapsulated by the somewhat awkward idea of a 'pluralism of discourses'. It hardly needs a name, for it is more important that it be done than that it be described.

This book very much takes the latter, wandering approach than it does the former, systematic approach. I am encouraged in this endeavour by the fact that while I have spent the whole of my life in or on the margins of the Christian community, I increasingly find myself surrounded by friends and acquaintances who are either indifferent about, or hostile to, God and religion in general. The topics treated here are in the main those which tend to arise again and again in conversations I have had over the years with friends, family, acquaintances, colleagues and students: questions such as the meaning of human suffering, the idea that God is nothing more than humanity writ large, the question of whether we can know anything beyond this world, the apparently unattractive character of the God of the Bible, the question of creation and its origin, and so on. The nature of many of these topics usually entails a fairly stringent critique of traditional ideas of God, and this fact may make some readers think that I err on the side of deconstruction and criticism, rather than on the side of constructive thought about God. Yet, while this is probably the case, the continued presence of the same few topics and issues about God raised by intelligent people who are not scholars of religion might indicate just how divorced from mainstream culture a great deal of theology has become. Either way, I will leave that to the reader to judge. This short book, therefore, does not even pretend to say everything about God (as if such a thing were possible). It does not pretend to defend any particular theology, least of all official Christian dogma. If there is a main theme it is that the idea of a God who is like us except much more powerful is no longer credible, and that we best understand God when we remain silent.

I have long been dissatisfied by both traditional theism and modernist atheism. Much of Christian 'systematic' theology treats God as unproblematic and chooses to bracket or simply ignore the truly staggering challenge which advances in the natural sciences offer to any supernatural account of the world and of human nature (some recent Christian theology even seeks to make a virtue out of this necessity and claims to be 'non-foundationalist', i.e. it does not have to justify its truth claims in any public way). But a purely naturalist account of our origins and of our nature is perfectly coherent and it would be a foolish theologian indeed who proceeded as if it were the year 1001 rather than 2001. As a colleague put it to me recently: 'Science does not make it impossible to believe, but it makes it easy not to.' On the other hand, atheism as an epistemological or ontological (not simply a methodological) statement about reality seems to me to go too far; it makes an epistemological claim that cannot be substantiated and does not do justice to the richness of the world's great religious traditions, or consider with adequate seriousness the evolutionary importance of religion for the development of human culture. It closes too quickly the door to the sacred. Too much atheistic criticism of religion (I am thinking of some prominent science writers) cannot seem to move beyond seeing religion as an impoverished cosmology or a defunct epistemology. While this limited viewpoint is often encouraged by some theologians, this is no reason to reduce religion, or 'God', to a dead branch on the tree of knowledge. My own position would best be described as 'religious naturalism', close to the views of Tillich and Drees discussed later. I believe that we must take with absolute seriousness, and as the starting-point for any reflection on religion, the fact that our presence on this planet is a matter of sheer contingency. Of course this hard fact (and it is a fact) does not preclude a religious explanation (such as a creator God) but it does not require it, and that piece of knowledge is a crucial difference between modern educated humans and our ancestors (or uneducated contemporaries) who had/have no such knowledge. As Dietrich Bonhoeffer put it, the world does not *need* God.

Nevertheless, the idea of God remains a powerful and real possibility for enriching our culture and our world. 'God' is the utterly ineffable symbol through which we attempt to express a reality greater than the fragments of the mundane, a totality greater than the self, and a horizon beyond the tangible. Philosophers might want to call this symbol a 'regulative concept' but this does not necessarily deny the possibility of it also being a real entity. Yet, we will never know if there is such an entity, a real Being, but this does not mean that we have to abandon all talk of 'God'. Putting the issue of God in terms of a simple dualist option ('Do you believe in God or not?') seems to me to mirror the worst tendencies of our culture to polarize and dichotomize (black/white, male/female, gay/straight, believer/unbeliever). Perhaps the cultural influence tentatively called 'postmodernity' has begun to blur the boundaries of these polarities, and in my view that can only be a good thing. So, in this book I consider 'God' as a radical possibility, always ahead of us, never within our grasp, always elusive, and never capable of finally being affirmed or denied. This might seem hopelessly liberal to some and mere religious nostalgia to others, yet it is, I think, a real possibility for transcendence in a fragmented culture.

Chapters 1 and 2 look at the impact on our individual selves and our culture when God can no longer be thought of in traditional ways. Chapter 3 treats of Christian negative theology, which is still a rich resource for thinking about God today: there were many great minds in less free situations than ours who thought of God in radical ways. Chapters 4 and 5 offer a critique of the anthropomorphic God and of the idea, prevalent in contemporary 'feel-good' Christianity, that you can somehow have the God of love without the less desirable characteristics which previous generations of Christians tended not to excise from God's nature. Chapters 6 and 7 critique the idea that you can gain a true revelation or know-ledge of God, either from history (the basis of most Christian doctrine) or from cosmology (a favourite issue in much contemporary theology). Chapter 8 offers some possibilities for thinking of God anew in our postmodern culture. The theses which make up the Conclusion could stand as a summary of the main points raised throughout the text.

Although I am in substantial agreement with feminism's critique of the God of patriarchy, I generally refer here to God as 'he' because, in the interests of accuracy, that is what the tradition I am discussing has done. Also, when I refer to God as a 'Being' (upper case) I am talking about the transcendent God as traditionally understood by monotheists; otherwise I speak of the 'being of God' (lower case) to refer to God's mode of existence; 'beings' in the lower case refers to entities in this world such as you and me. All biblical quotations are from the *HarperCollins Study Bible* (New Revised Standard Version).

I am very grateful to several of my academic colleagues who have either read part of the text or discussed particular issues with me: in a very busy world, Ronald Begley, Alain Brizard, John Izzi, Paul Murray, Ray Patterson and Jeff Trumbower all gave their time and attention. Thanks also to Robin Baird-Smith at Continuum for his patience. Most of all I am indebted to my wife Cecilia Redmond for her indefatigable support and encouragement and her critical comment on all of the text.

On 2 March 2001, just as I was completing the manuscript for this book, John Diamond, the writer whose views on God and suffering are discussed in Chapter 5, died of cancer, age 47.

1

God and the Self

Little Fly
Thy summers play,
My thoughtless hand
Has brushed away.
Am not I
A fly like thee?
Or art not thou
A man like me?
(William Blake, 'The Fly',
from *Songs of Innocence and
Experience*, 1970 [1789/1794])

But in the eyes of God, the infinite spirit, all the millions
that have lived and now live do not make a crowd. He
only sees each individual. (Søren Kierkegaard, *The
Diary of Søren Kierkegaard*, 1960, s. 127)

Since the origins of human culture, more has been written
and said about God than about virtually any other topic. In
the great monotheistic religions alone, not only the Hebrew
and Christian Bibles and the Koran, but tens of thousands of
theological, philosophical, liturgical, spiritual and devotional
works have been created to attempt to grasp, explain, invoke,
implore or reject and refute this most elusive of all concepts.
The fascination of human beings with our origins, with the

marvellous universe about which we now know so much, with
the mysteries of consciousness and of our own deaths, means
that reflection on the possibility of God, of the prospect of an
ultimate ground giving meaning to all of this, is unlikely to
ever cease. Even the atheist is caught within this web of
divine possibilities, for the atheist defines herself and her
view of life, partly at least, in terms of a Being which she
thinks of as non-existing. In the Western world the question
of the meaning or purpose of the universe and of our existence in it is encapsulated by the question of God, even if the
answer given to that question is to reject God as merely a tes-
timony to the creative power of the human imagination.
Fascination with God is not easily erased.

To believe in God as classically conceived by the Jewish
and Christian religions is to believe in the (almost) impossible. A divine Being, invisible and intangible yet capable of
acting on matter; closer to us than we are to ourselves, yet
infinitely transcending all that is human; the maker of each
of us in the divine image and likeness, yet also passionately
partisan in love and war; all-loving yet permitting a world of
evil, pain and suffering; all-knowing and all-powerful, yet
permitting free will (or not, depending on your theology);
Yahweh Sabaoth ('God of the armies') who knocks down the
walls of Jericho and enables Joshua to commit genocide
against the inhabitants, 'men and women, young and old, as
well as oxen, sheep and asses' (Joshua 6.21) also implores us
to do right, love goodness and walk humbly with him (Micah
6.8); the impassive and serene God of the philosophers who
has all the qualities of philosophical perfection is also the
living, threatening, consoling, vengeful, angry, beseeching
God of Cain and Abel, Moses, Ezekiel and Job. He is also, lest
we forget, the fatherly *Abba* of the rabbis and of Jesus of
Nazareth, who himself, according to Christian orthodoxy, is
also God, the second person of the divine Trinity.

Who could have conceived such a Being? From where could

such a strange combination of ideas have come? On one level the answer to this question is easy. Historians and scholars of religion have analysed and documented the changing ideas of the divine from the earliest polytheism in the Bible to the emergence of monotheism in Israel to the doctrinal defini-tions of early Christianity. One of the reasons that there are many images of God in the Hebrew Bible is that originally there were many gods; from this polytheism of tribal deities emerged monotheism – the idea that there is only one God for the whole world – and from this again came the Christian development that God is revealed to be three-in-one.

Scholars of religion have long been aware of the way in which Greek philosophy, in particular the neo-platonic philo-sophy of late antiquity, influenced the Christian concept of God and led to the tension which exists between the so-called 'God of the philosophers' and the God of the Bible, the apparent paradox of a divine being who is simultaneously and eternally both impassive and personal, the latter quality requiring some level of compassion, empathy or love not easily reconciled with the *apatheia* of a Supreme Being or Unmoved Mover. In purely historical and anthropological terms we now have a treasure of historical knowledge not only about the origins of Judaism, Christianity and Islam but also about the religious tenets and concepts of the divine found in the belief-systems of indigenous peoples; we even have a reasonable idea of the role which religion may have played in the lives of our earliest *homo sapiens* ancestors (see Ehrlich, 2000, pp. 213–21).

Nietzsche – and in this he is followed by much modern and postmodern thought – believed that an historical explanation was enough to dismiss for ever the need for God. When the historical origins of belief are established it is no longer nec-essary to disprove God's existence; when we know the mundane historical origins of an idea we are free to allow it to drift away into historical oblivion. But the historical explanation offers us an answer to the 'How?' question; it does not answer the question 'Why?' Why should the idea of the divine become so powerful in the first place? For that 'Why?' answer we have a range of possibilities. We have theories which tell us that God is the projection of our highest human aspirations (Feuerbach), the guarantor of social conformity and cohesion (Durkheim), consolation for the powerlessness produced by our alienation from the product of our labour (Marx), a cultural invention which allows the revenge of the weak against the strong (Nietzsche), and after Freud we have a surfeit of psychological and pseudo-psychological explanations of the origin, role and function of God in the human psyche.

Then, not least, we have the classical theological answers. The Catholic tradition of Christianity has defended the concept of God as an idea planted in us by God; our concept of the divine is natural to human beings because it is itself a revelation from God accessible through the powers of human reason, to be complemented by other, special revelations about the divine nature (e.g. as three-in-one), salvation (e.g. as accomplished by the atoning death of Jesus of Nazareth), an afterlife (e.g. the bodily resurrection), and so on; these special revelations are accessible only through the eyes of faith. This is the approach to God defended by Thomas Aquinas, and it can be found in various manifestations in modern Catholic theology. A different emphasis can be found among churches and theologians influenced by Luther and Calvin's critique of the use of reason in theological speculation. All knowledge of God is possible only through the gift of faith; the divine can only be encountered when we are confronted by the Word of God uttered in the salvific encounter with the risen Christ; apart from this, all religious words are merely human words. In modern theology this view is most closely associated with the twentieth-century Swiss theologian Karl Barth.

To discuss each of these approaches separately would merit a book, or indeed many books. But here my concern is not with adjudicating the merits and demerits of these various theories about God; even less am I interested in rehearsing the often acrimonious disputes between Christian theologians about the nature of revelation. Rather, I want to ask about the value of the idea of God, about its worth or lack of worth to us human beings. My premise here is simple: the question of God is not one which can be answered by philosophical or theological argument; proofs and disproofs do not work, and the truth will always elude our feeble attempts at certainty. Yet unless there is at hand an unexpected and unambiguous divine revelation about which we can all agree, then it is we mortals who are left to struggle with the questions about the origin and meaning of our world and ourselves, with the possibility or not of a God who gives coherence to it all. It is we, here and now, each with our particular culture, language, gender, genetic make-up and psychological disposition who have to try to ask about the value and purpose of our lives. We cannot step outside our world and view it *sub specie aeternitatis*; that, after all, is the prerogative of God, and we have no such luxury.

It follows that the answers we give will always be our answers, they will bear the imprint of our needs, concerns and hopes; they will be answers which we find pragmatic and useful to make sense of the existence in which we find ourselves. Even those religious believers who think that their truth is the final truth to which everyone should cleave will have to admit this much: the religious beliefs which they hold to be true should be useful for human beings, should contribute to the fulfilment of legitimate human aspirations and should offer us some hope of discerning, albeit always inadequately, the meaning of being a person here and now with this one life to live. But where we lack the confidence of the true believer, we have to ask the pragmatic question first:

what value does the idea of God offer me here and now to make sense of this life that I am living in this world and at this time?

One thing should be clear, however: to ask the question of God in this way is not a matter of weighing up the good or evil done by religious people the world over. Bertrand Russell, that doyen of atheists, thought that one of the reasons religion should be discarded was that it had done very little good and a great deal of harm. This argument might be convincing if it were in any way verifiable, but it is not. Religions have indeed done a great deal of harm and many atrocities have been and continue to be committed in the name of God, but for every Torquemada there has been a Francis of Assisi, for every war-mongering mullah there are many more peaceful and devout Muslims, and thankfully there seem to be more people inclined to be like Mother Teresa than like Jim Jones. Even though for each of us individually our direct experience of religion will greatly influence our view of God (after all, someone abused by a member of the clergy may understandably find it difficult to believe in a loving Father in heaven), this attempt to judge God by the good and evil done by religious believers is not a viable way to answer the question as a whole, because we have no way to ever weigh up the balance of the good over and against the evil.

But what about more sustained and serious attacks on the idea of God, such as the charge that belief in God destroys human freedom? In 1945, the then-renowned French philosopher Jean-Paul Sartre delivered a lecture at the Club Maintenant in Paris which was later published as *Existentialism and Humanism*. Sartre's aim was to defend existentialist philosophy and atheism, which he claimed could not be separated from a real understanding of the human condition. He intended to clarify what he meant by the term 'existentialism', which he admitted was used so loosely at the time as to hardly have any fixed meaning, and to respond to some critics from the left (the French Communists) and from the right (the French Catholics). In particular he wished to dispense with the view that existentialism is a pessimistic doctrine which leads to despair through its over-emphasis on the 'evil side of human life' (Sartre, 1980, p. 24) and its apparent capitulation to moral relativism.

Sartre's argument against God has its origins in his understanding of human freedom. Following the analysis of the human being as a being-in-the-world (*Dasein*) presented by Martin Heidegger in the originating text of twentieth-century existentialism, *Being and Time* (1962 [1927]), Sartre criticizes classical Western thought, and Christianity in particular, for the way in which it has focused on a fixed 'essence' of the human, to which each individual person is then expected to conform. Thus, for example, orthodox Christianity holds a view of the human being as created in the image and likeness of God, tainted by sin yet redeemed by Christ, and capable of everlasting life with God. From the perspective of traditional Christian orthodoxy this human nature holds for all people at all times and in all places. However, in the opinion of Sartre, this idea of there being fixed elements to human nature is actually destructive of human freedom because it prevents the individual human person from engaging in a free and creative exploration of the possibilities inherent in their own life; it prohibits us from fully taking responsibility for our own 'existence'.

So Sartre, interpreting Heidegger, wished to invert the traditional way in which the Western world had conceived of human freedom. In place of the idea that our individual existence should be formed from responsible use of freedom in the framework of the essence of human nature common to us all, Sartre believed that there is no fixed essence to the human being and that we are therefore forced to create our own essence through free choice of the values we pursue in the course of our existence. In short, if the classical view is that our existence follows our essence, for the existentialists our essence must follow our existence because we have no fixed nature to begin with; we must each create our own essence from the circumstances of our individual lives. As we are not defined in advance by God or nature, we find ourselves cast into the world. In Heidegger's phrase, we experience life as a 'thrown-ness' (German *geworfenheit*) which brings us face to face with the question of the nature of our being. We are thereby compelled to accept responsibility for our own values and identity. We are nothing more than what we make of ourselves.

To illustrate his point, Sartre compares the human being as conceived in the mind of God with the idea of a paper-knife as conceived in the mind of a craftsman. The knife has a defined purpose and it is designed to follow a particular course of action and to fulfil the function implicit in that design. Sartre sees no difference between this and the human being as created by God; if God exists, then we are created with a certain fixed nature and purpose, and our freedom is circumscribed within the limits set by the 'essence' of humanity as defined by God. But this cannot be called true freedom because it already sets limits to what the human being can be. It is only if we deny God that we can reject the idea of a fixed, pre-determined human essence and acknowledge that we are fully capable of creating our own notion of human nature. So, he says:

> If it is true that existence is prior to essence, man is responsible for what he is. Thus, the first effect of existentialism is that it puts every man in possession of himself as he is, and places the entire responsibility for his existence squarely upon his own shoulders. (Sartre, 1980, p. 29)

In this new situation we have freedom forced upon us and cannot escape; in Sartre's vivid and striking formulation, we are 'condemned to be free'.

Sartre is well aware that the immediate issue which this gives rise to is the question posed by the nineteenth-century Russian novelist Fyodor Dostoevsky in *The Brothers Kara-mazov*: if God does not exist, then is everything permitted? After all, both the idea of a benevolent creator deity who has made us in the divine image and likeness, and the secular counterpart of this in the idea of an established and determined human nature both provide a rationale for behaving morally. For example, both Christian morality, which commands us that we must love one another because God has loved us first, and the moral philosophy of Immanuel Kant, which sees all rational beings as capable of knowing the universal moral law and adhering to it, provide us with a pre-existing framework which sets limits to our freedom to pursue our own interests irrespective of the costs to others. But if we are condemned to be free and have no human nature determined in advance, then why should we not choose to be liars, thieves, racists and murderers if that is what most effectively gets us what we would desire? After all, with no God to look over us and no nature to determine us, are we not free to be and do whatsoever we wish?

Sartre's response to this problem is to re-introduce a form of universalism after all. He claims that when we choose to act on our freedom we do not choose for ourselves as individuals, but by implication we choose for all others; when we decide on our chosen path, we infer, says Sartre, that this is the best path for all others as well. As one of his examples, Sartre picks the practice of marrying and having children; if I take this option, he says, 'I am thereby committing not only myself, but humanity as a whole, to the practice of monogamy' (1980, p. 30). Now it does not take much insight to see that this is an inconsistent and indeed untenable position. I can easily imagine people who are themselves committed to monogamy while acknowledging the rights of others to engage in different kinds of sexual relationships: polygamy, androgyny, promiscuity, homosexuality, or celibacy. In fact, Sartre's position seems less a recipe for individual freedom than one for coercion and control, for in the absence of any counterbalancing moral principle (such as respect for the inherent dignity of other persons and cultures) what is to prevent me, should I have the power in some dark imaginary future, to impose monogamy on the whole population?

Sartre is forced into this inconsistency by his need to respond to the accusation that the existentialist emphasis on moral subjectivity will lead to moral relativism, and to avoid that charge he resorts to a Kantian ethic of sorts, a universal principle for which he can provide no grounding other than his own assertion that it is so. Yet there is no reason whatsoever why it should be the case that I am implicitly recommending my behaviour to every other person, as the example of marriage shows. Further, as Kant was aware, it can sometimes be in a person's interests to encourage others to behave morally while they themselves exploit this to their own advantage by.breaking the moral code. So, what if my decision is to marry a rich person and then kill them to inherit their wealth? Am I thereby recommending this to everyone, even my own next spouse? Sartre's response was that I only ever choose what is good and thereby imply that it is the good for all (1980, p. 29).

However, any course of action pursued by any individual person may well be termed 'good' by that person, but it does not automatically follow, as Sartre claims, that that notion of 'good' defined in this way can bear a universal value. Here Sartre is simply conflating the use of the word 'good' to describe an individual's evaluation of their own actions, with a prescriptive meaning of 'good' as referring to values which carry universal meaning; for it is clear that what I may consider to be 'good' for me (robbing my local bank, say) can be far from 'good' for other people. In the end, Sartre's theory becomes untenable and is reduced to tautologies.

However, Sartre's critique is of great significance in helping us to understand the rejection of religion among large sections of the population in Western countries, because it has become a dogma of Western atheism that belief in God is incompatible with human freedom and this has seeped into the cultural fabric of many Western societies. Yet the high aspirations of twentieth-century existentialism to empower the individual to be free of all constraint in the fashioning of our own lives seem now almost quaint, as we have become increasingly conscious of the cultural, social, psychological and, above all, economic forces which influence our lives every day. Anyone who owns a television set or reads a daily newspaper cannot but be aware of the extent to which individuals in modern Western capitalist societies have become objects of manipulation by corporations, advertisers, spin-doctors, special interest groups, leisure providers and governments. At the beginning of the twentieth century our freedom seems less threatened by God than by the very social forces which also, ironically, make our societies so vibrant and 'successful'. So Sartre was wrong: there is no reason why one cannot be a free moral person and believe in God; and, conversely, it is perfectly possible to be a moral person without believing in God. This granted, the question of how the human self can be thought of in relation to what we might call 'God' remains to be thought out.

A more gainful approach to the question of ascertaining the value of the idea of God for human beings is suggested by the philosopher Roger Scruton. Scruton proposes the idea that the human person, aware of her situation as both an object in nature with other objects and at the same time a conscious subject who can look at the world of nature to some extent from 'outside', experiences this subject–object tension as a form of estrangement (this idea goes back to Hegel), of 'metaphysical loneliness' (Scruton, 1996, p. 89). As sociologists and anthropologists have endlessly pointed out, religious rituals, myths and acts of worship function to bring individuals together to forge a powerful sense of community (the word 'religion' has its etymological roots in the Latin 'to bind') and Scruton suggests that this should be understood not merely in sociological but also in metaphysical terms: religious acts are the acts of subjects, coming together to enact a ritual which places the worshipping community beyond the world of mere objects and offers a transcendental perspective on the world to which we also belong as objects. This allows us to imaginatively conceive of an ultimate transcendental perspective, one in which the observer does not also have to belong to (and eventually return to) the world of objects.

For Scruton this perspective is the perspective of God, specifically the God of monotheism who, as the creator of nature, is not a part of nature, and who encapsulates both the eternal and the personal perspective. In religious ritual, thinks Scruton, we perceive in an imperfect manner something of the divine viewpoint and we are momentarily raised to the level of the transcendent. Although he does not make this connection, this is precisely the theology of the divine liturgy as it is understood by the Christian Eastern Orthodox churches: in worship we participate already in the divine life, we anticipate a little bit of heaven here on earth, and we truly know the transcendent. In these moments our estrangement is healed, our subjectivity is revealed and the promise of an eternal union with the divine is held out to us.

Of course all of this can only be seen through the eyes of faith and, in its most intense form, through the sublime experience of the mystic. Faith here is then understood, in Scruton's words, as 'a supreme overcoming of our transcendental loneliness' (1996, p. 95). In acts of worship we are raised above ourselves into communion with other subjects and with the transcendent. We are fleetingly lifted out of the mundane and into the holy. However, notwithstanding the special character of the God of monotheism as a subject who stands both with and also over and against our own subject-ivity, this intensity of experience in which the religious ritual functions to overcome our alienation from the world and to heal the estrangement we sense between our selves as subjects and as objects in the world, is surely available to all religions, and not just those which espouse monotheism. It may also be just as readily available in intense experiences, such as art, dancing, music, sports or sex, activities which we do not normally consider 'religious'. While the cultivation of an intensity of experience can be an effect of religious activity, particularly for the great religious mystics, religion is not the only vehicle through which our estrangement from the world can be overcome.

Yet the orthodox Christian concept of God, which attempts to keep in balance both the personal face of God and the divine otherness and transcendence, has the capacity to offer us an experience of wholeness, even – to use a specifically theological term – an experience of redemption. In an encounter with a reality which we perceive as both personal and yet infinitely beyond, we can see ourselves as saved from our estrangement, not simply in some otherworldly sense, but also in the sense of a here-and-now healing, a momentary displacement out of the ordinary world of being one object among others. For those who believe, their belief is itself a transcending reality, a glimpse into a possibility which is always more than the merely mundane.

Yet, in a context in which more and more of us find it diffi-cult to conceive of a God who exists outside the world and acts on it as a person acts in and on the natural world, how are we to think of this encounter with a reality which lifts us out of ourselves? Is this something done by an all-powerful yet personal Being, rewarding those who attend religious ritual with a sense of the self as healed and redeemed? Are we left to try to argue with and convince ourselves that such a Being is really there and really cares? Or are we left to contemplate the mystery of our own encounter with the transcendent as an encounter between our everyday self and the sacred that we are capable of? Like Saint Augustine, we are impelled to go inward into the self, for there dwells the truth; but this time it is not necessarily an encounter between the abject self and the divine holiness but an encounter of the self with its own depths and with its own possibility.

But is this not a deception? Does not the redemptive encounter with the transcendent require belief in a God external to the world? Not necessarily, although, against those anti-religionists who can see no value in any reference to God, I cannot see any harm in understanding the religious experience in this way. First, as we have discussed, the idea of an ontologically real divine Being with analogous human characteristics acting on and interfering in this world is regarded as unbelievable by millions of modern people, but does this mean that religious experience becomes impossible? Not at all, for such experiences are *our* experiences and are not conditional on belief in the God of monotheism, even less on more specific beliefs such as the Christian belief in a triune God. Second, we are well aware that both the dominant religions of the world and the indigenous religions of thousands of different human cultures allow for such experiences; they are no less real or legitimate than an experience which is founded on an encounter with the God of Judaism, Islam or Christianity.

Even more interestingly, is it not the case that our interest in the relationship between God and the self and between the self and the world is merely another instance of our Western fixation on the individual? Is it not the case that the encounter with the God of monotheism – that ultimate self-sufficient male figure – acts either to obliterate the self (as in the emphasis which some branches of Christianity have placed on the corruption of human nature when compared with the infinite majesty of God), or perhaps our more contemporary failing, that the encounter with God is used to legitimize our current wishes, desires and self-identity, so that God becomes merely the guarantor of our own subjective certainty? Is it that we are either beaten into submission like Jacob's futile attempt to overcome the angel with whom he wrestled, or that we, like Descartes, reach our own certainties first and then use God to ground them? This latter possibility is a dangerous one, and not only in the personal but also in the political realm, for God is a malleable concept and we have no shortage of examples of the divine being invoked to justify this or that political viewpoint.

Here, however, we are concerned with the self, and with the question of what it can mean for the self to have an encounter with or experience of God, when God is not necessarily understood as a superior Being which exists external to the world. Is it possible for us to contemplate this as a valuable and rewarding possibility, a worthwhile spiritual path for us to take, or is it simply another delusion, another lie we tell ourselves to make ourselves feel better? The answer to this depends in the end, I believe, not only on our concept of God, but also and fundamentally on our concept of the self. As long as we understand the self as the centre of location of an autonomous ego, independent and distinct from everything else, then we are left alone and isolated, fending for ourselves in a world of self-contained selves. In late modernity and into the contemporary period this notion of the autonomous self has come in for much criticism, some of it (as in French philosopher Michel Foucault's famously apocalyptic proclamation of the 'death of man') exaggerated and somewhat far-fetched, other elements (as in the feminist critique of the male ideal as the human archetype) a legitimate and necessary corrective to distorted concepts of autonomy. The feminist critique in particular has helped us to understand the relational nature of our human selves: we do not create our individual selves and characters *ex nihilo*, we are rather created by a network of relations (parents, family, friendships, nation, language, culture, lovers, enemies, children, and so on).

It is important that feminism has helped us to reappraise our understanding of the human person, yet, as a critique which occurs *within* the parameters of Western notions of individual identity, it still leaves us with the fundamental problem of how to understand ourselves at the deepest level; and here, I think, we Westerners can learn something from the Buddhist concept of the self. Buddhists do not think of the self as an autonomous entity, or even as a single entity created by a network of relations. Rather, the self is itself nothing more than the product or construct of a complex set of relations; it is a phenomenon created by means of what is known in the Middle Way (*Madhyamika*) school of Buddhist thought as the notion of 'dependent origination'. In this way of thinking of the self, and indeed of all reality, nothing can be reduced to a single explanation or essence; everything – including the sense of self which you and I call consciousness – is dependent for its identity on other factors which are themselves dependent, and so on. In a recent work, the present Dalai Lama explains the concept of dependent origination as occurring on three levels. First, in terms of cause and effect, nothing comes into existence or remains in existence solely by itself; everything is related to and dependent upon a web of other causes and conditions. Second, there is a mutual dependency between the parts and the whole of any entity; what we call the 'whole' is itself dependent upon the parts, which are themselves made up of other parts. Third, all things are defined in terms of their relations: a parent is a parent by virtue of his/her children, a farmer is so by virtue of his/her work; identities are created by means of mutual dependence (Dalai Lama, 1999, pp. 35–47).

This extends as far as the consciousness which you and I identify with the 'self', for as the Dalai Lama expresses it, 'if all phenomena are dependent on other phenomena, and if no phenomena can exist independently, even our most cherished selves must be considered not to exist in the way we normally assume' (p. 41). There is no single characteristic by which I might identify my own 'self', as if I could say 'There, I have identified what it is'. Rather, my 'self' is constituted by my relationships, not in the sense of this being a past event (as in our parents' or our school's influence on our development) but in terms of an ongoing reality. My 'self' is what I am in terms of how I am constituted by my past, my present and my future relations with others and with the world.

I would emphasize that this idea is not intended as a literal declaration that there is no 'I'; that would be absurd and a gross misrepresentation. On the other hand, neither am I suggesting that we need to regard this concept of the self as unproblematic or that we need to accept the position of any one school of Buddhist metaphysics. It is, rather, a very useful corrective to our Western view of the self as an independent entity, which tends to remain even after we have corrected its worst manifestations (as the feminist critique of patriarchy has done). This view of the self, as constituted in an ongoing way through a complex web of interactions and as a never-completed project, offers us a rich source of possibilities for thinking of our personal, social, political and religious identities and relations. When we think of what it means for someone to be Bolivian or Bangladeshi, Christian or Hindu, female or male, gay or straight, and think of it in terms of all of our identities being dependent, we cannot but begin to think in terms of barriers being broken down, of our interests being not always in conflict. I can no longer think of 'myself' as if I were an autonomous being cut off from other autonomous beings, no longer think of my religion as a self-contained entity which guards the truth jealously, no longer think of my relations in terms of opposites (sexual, political, national or religious) and no longer think of my relation to God as that between two independent selves, the one a weak and pale imitation of the Other.

In the early part of the nineteenth century, the first great modern theologian, Friedrich Schleiermacher, attempted to redefine the Christian experience in terms comprehensible to those people who took seriously Kant's critique of the powers of human reason (see Chapter 2). Kant had set out the limits of human reason: reason cannot step outside the bounds of experience to give an account of the being or nature of the divinity. God, for Kant, becomes simply a transcendental ideal, useful for moral purposes but not something which we can entertain as the object of knowledge.

Responding to Kant's critique and to Johann Fichte's criticism of the application of anthropomorphic categories to God, Schleiermacher realized that we can no longer think of theological statements as statements about God as such; they are rather statements about ourselves and our religious spirit:

> You will not consider it blasphemy, I hope, that belief in God depends on the direction of the imagination. You will know that imagination is the highest and most original element in us, and that everything besides it is merely reflection on it; you will know that it is your imagination that creates the world for you, and that you can have no God without the world. (Schleiermacher, 1988 [1799], p. 138)

Schleiermacher defined the quintessential religious experience as an experience of 'absolute dependency' where religious believers experience themselves as depending on an utterly gracious reality beyond themselves, which Christians and others name God. For non-believers, of course, if they experience this sense of dependence, it is simply their awareness of their place in the natural world. Schleiermacher's notion of the dependent self is, however, still circumscribed within the Western idea of the self as a separate entity, standing over and against the ultimate transcendental reality and dependent upon it. However, if – partly due to Kant, Fichte and Schleiermacher – we can no longer so easily conceptualize God as a Being which exists external to the world, and independent of it, then we can think of our feeling of dependence as essentially an inner-worldly reality, expressing our sense of relatedness to all of reality (including 'God'), and experiencing that relatedness as gracious.

I suggest that the Buddhist notion of the self which I have briefly outlined can help us to expand and deepen Schleiermacher's theological insight. When the self is itself understood as completely dependent and God is no longer thought of as an all-powerful transcendental being, we no longer need to think of the relation of the self to God in terms of the creature and the Creator, the sinner and the perfect One, the finite and the infinite, the contingent and the necessary; this oppositional way of thinking is what led us in the first place to the battle to rid ourselves of this overbearing God and is the root of the development of atheism.

We are now free to think of the relation of the self to the whole of reality in terms of my existence as something which is given to me, not necessarily by a transcendent God who stands over and against me, but by the graciousness of the reality by means of which I am constituted; I have been created by the world of which I am a part, and my life can be understood as a gift. Unlike the external God who could accept nothing back except obedience, having all perfection already, I can give a great deal back in terms of my interaction with the world and the other beings with whom I am interdependent. I can experience all of reality as 'absolute dependence' and be thankful for it.

Our religious experience then becomes a relation not to some other Being but to the depths of our own being. This, as I have emphasized, is not now to be understood as merely the individual exploring her or his own autonomous consciousness; I am not referring here to simply a psychological event, but rather an orientation towards the whole of human existence which regards that existence as constituted by relationality. This orientation does not require us to be members of particular religious communities, nor does it require special training or esoteric insight, although it might well be a skill which can be cultivated. It requires only that we abandon the reified and objectified concepts of both God and self which can no longer serve us well, and enter into the depths of the experience of what it means to be a creature dependent on other creatures not only for my physical existence but also for the identity of what I call my 'self'. If we can do that, and do it well, then we could, perhaps, move not beyond but through our metaphysical estrangement.

Then, we might even claim to have experienced God as personal. But not as personal in the sense of knowing the nature of a transcendent Being existing independently of us and about whom we can only speak through inadequate use of human analogical terms. Rather, we can speak of God as personal because we ourselves are personal beings whose relation to the whole of reality is constitutive of our personhood. For each of us, this life which we live is constituted by our relation to the world which produced us, a world of material bodies, animate and inanimate matter, other persons and whole societies of human beings, with all the mass of cultural symbolism this produces. In reaching into the depths of the experience of what it means to be a person in *this* world, and not in some world to come, we can perhaps on occasion venture to say that we have encountered God.

To understand the world as giving me my 'self', and to understand my 'self' in conjunction with other 'selves' as beings capable of understanding that world and thereby giving meaning to the activities and lives of ourselves, is in the words of biologist Ursula Goodenough, 'to articulate a covenant with Mystery' (1998, p. 167). Such a covenant with Mystery is not an agreement brokered in fear with an other-worldly Being; it is not something which is made with only one person on behalf of one people and which when broken angers and offends the deity; it is not something which requires external divine intervention due to our own inadequacies, and it is not something which awaits the end of time for the full realization of its promise. This is the covenant which we make with ourselves and with our world; it stems not from external divine intervention but from our own understanding of our place in nature and in the interpersonal world in which 'we live and move and have our being' (Acts 17.28). To make this covenant with Mystery is not to pretend to have all the answers, religious or metaphysical; it is not to assume that we few have been the fortunate ones, born into the divinely chosen community. It is rather to be able to celebrate our sheer good fortune in being here at all, whatever the explanation. It is to be able to say: 'Hosannah! Not in the highest, but right here, right now, this' (Goodenough, 1998, p. 168).

2

The Sickness Unto Death?

It is not without profound sorrow that one admits to oneself that in their highest flights the artists of all ages have raised to heavenly transfiguration precisely those conceptions which we now recognize as false: they are the glorifiers of the religious and philosophical errors of mankind . . . (Friedrich Nietzsche, *Human, All Too Human*, 1987 [1878])

In 1793, Immanuel Kant's *Religion Within the Limits of Reason Alone* expressed a view of religious belief consistent with the great philosopher's austere evaluation of the powers of human reason. In matters of religion, he said, the *minimum* of knowledge must suffice; that is, all that we may subjectively hold as knowledge is that the existence of God is possible (Kant, 1960 [1793], p. 142). The aim of Kant's theory of knowledge was to delineate for ever that which can rightly be called knowledge from judgements which rely on faith or on mere opinion. In his view his philosophy was establishing the autonomy of human reason and laying the epistemological foundations for scientific knowledge. At the same time he endeavoured to compensate for the critique of knowledge in the sphere of religion by placing belief on a new footing of subjective resolution, free from that misplaced confidence in reason which had marked the attempts by both Catholic and Protestant Christianity to demonstrate the existence of God through 'proofs' or other forms of rational argument.

One hundred years after Kant, towards the end of the nineteenth century, the veiled implication of Kant's view of religion, namely that the *maximum* we could expect from reflection on religion was the mere possibility of the existence of God, had come to rule the consciousness of European intellectual life. But in the tenor of the times, this maximum possibility for religion seemed hardly worth taking seriously, so little did it appear to serve the needs and aspirations of the confident nineteenth century. Of course churches continued to baptize, marry, and bury the dead, but among many of the educated the divine had withered away, to the extent that the possible existence of God was a very weak hypothesis indeed, leaving only the functions of the churches as a reminder of the Christian culture which had for so long been synonymous with the identity of the West. To many intellectuals of the nineteenth century, even some theologians, God was a dead branch on the tree of knowledge, and cultural and intellectual life could only fully flourish once this defunct accretion had been pruned from the minds of modern women and men. As Matthew Arnold put it in 'Dover Beach' (Arnold, 1994), all that could be heard of the once mighty sea of faith was its 'melancholy, long, withdrawing roar'.

This, at least, is the conventional story, retold in different ways and with some enthusiasm by many writers since. A. N. Wilson's recent work *God's Funeral* (1999) is a case in point. Wilson takes his title from Thomas Hardy's eponymous poem in which the author imagines himself attending the funeral of God, who is laid to rest by the great and the good. The poet feels the loss but cannot comfort the mourners or support their faith. Moved with sympathy and struck speechless by the enormity of the event, the poet remembers his own, now absent, belief:

I did not forget
That what was mourned for, I, too, long had prized.

Death, we know, is final. So the poet, in a dazed and puzzled state, can only follow the cortège to the final resting place of God.

The perspective which Wilson takes on God's demise in an otherwise thorough and interesting book is instructive, for the long tale he tells is wedged between revealing passages, 'bookends' so to speak, which reveal almost as much as the main text itself. In the Preface he points out the obvious: God has not gone away, but is with us still. Where? Why, in intolerance and crassness of course; in the holy wars of the Ayatollahs, in the conservative views of evangelical Christians on politics and sexual ethics, in the special pleading of US President Bill Clinton for God's forgiveness for his peccadilloes. That this is the contemporary face of God seems obvious to Wilson and he greets it with a metaphorical shrug; why not try anything which works for you? Over 350 pages later, Wilson comes to the end of his chronicle and seems genuinely surprised that what he calls 'the Christian thing' has survived intact through to the end of the twentieth century. He refers fleetingly to a few 'world-changing men and women' such as Simone Weil (the only woman mentioned), Dietrich Bonhoeffer, Martin Luther King and John Paul II; these outstanding figures, he opines, 'decided to ignore the death of God in the nineteenth century' (Wilson, 1999, p. 354) and carry on regardless.

What is notable about this juxtaposition of the 'bad' presence of God and the 'good' presence of God, of intolerance versus heroism, is not the obvious over-simplification, but the fact that it suggests to us that Wilson has told only part of the story; the eclipse of God in the minds of the intellectual classes in modernity is only one act of the drama, for it does not explain the uncanny survival of God in ways both acceptable and unacceptable to modern sensibilities. The death of God has been greatly exaggerated, yet Wilson chooses to tell once again the tale of the putative death and not of the remarkable survival. It should be clear to any discerning observer of our contemporary world that God is still alive, even if this is often most evident in reactionary groups of various hues. God's continued presence in our world, in ways which appear both good and bad to sceptical observers like Wilson, makes it all the more intriguing to look into the rumours of his death.

If philosophers are sometimes reliable guides to the spirit of the age, then the story of the 'death' of God in the nineteenth century is best told by reference to Kant, Hegel and Nietzsche. However, while Nietzsche was the first to recognize fully the true meaning and consequences of the demise of God within significant quarters of Western society and culture, the seeds of the epochal shift which he perceived had been sown in the preceding centuries. The possibilities of atheism first emerged from within Christian thought itself, when in the early modern period of the late sixteenth and seventeenth centuries the defence of God by Christian theology became a rational project aimed at justifying Christianity before the bar of reason. When this occurred, belief in God became a matter of dispute, separated out from the depth structure of faith in which it could only be rightly comprehended. God became an optional possibility for explaining the world and the specifics of Christian belief came to be of secondary importance to the rational explanation of the power of the Creator.

In this context, the factors which made Christianity specifically Christian began to be played down for apologetic reasons. Christian theologians, anxious to prove that Christianity was a rational religion, placed less emphasis on elements of the Christian myth which were more difficult to defend philosophically: a deep concept of creation in which God is intimately involved in the world; an understanding of God as Trinity, with all the mystical connotations which that implies; the specific revelatory power of the salvation story told in the incarnation, death and resurrection of Jesus, and the consequences of that for our understanding of the human person and of history as a whole. These central beliefs did not disappear, but they took a back seat to the cognitive question of the possibility of belief in a Supreme Being. God came to be perceived primarily as an outside causative force which, as an explanatory cause, would eventually give way to the forces inherent in the universe itself, unveiled by the successes of the scientific method.

If God died in the nineteenth century, signs of his illness were present in the seventeenth and eighteenth centuries. Deism, with its confidence in the wisdom of the Supreme Creator and its disdain for any divine revelation other than that which is evident from the clever construction of the natural world, reduced the meaning of God to God's role as the Great Architect of creation. In the emergence in these centuries of the distant deistic God, whose role as creator was to start a world governed by natural laws, we have another significant factor in the process which would culminate in Nietzsche's proclamation of the death of God in the nineteenth century. God becomes distant from the creation to the point of separation, so that the creation can be perceived as continuing without divine intervention. But this deist perspective of God as First Cause, and little more, was far removed from the Christian concept of God's relation to the world which was based on an intimate engagement of Creator and creation. As Louis Dupré has expressed it in his outstanding study of the topic, 'never never before the modern age did Christians consider a notion of extrinsic causality adequate to express the intimate, permanent presence of God to his creation' (1993, p. 173). That is to say, it is only with the beginnings of modernity that a God who acts from afar as a cause outside the world becomes separated from the particularities of Christian belief, and a parallel separation of faith from nature develops.

Christianity discovered that from a God without Christ, without sacraments, without prayer and without hope, it is but a short step to a nature without God, for when God is so distant as to be absent, what is the difference between nature with God and nature without God? The connection between the natural world and its perceived divine origin, the core belief of deism, was further undermined by David Hume's penetrating critique of the design argument in his *Dialogues Concerning Natural Religion* (1990 [1779]). Hume argued that the analogy between the world as we know it and the mind of a single benign deity has no rational basis; the world might well be the creation of many gods or none, and we have no reason to draw any conclusion about the origin of the world from the way we find it. Eventually nature can be understood as existing without divine aid or intervention, and naturalism can replace the explanatory power of religion. At the origins of modernity, the philosophical counterpart to naturalism is the philosophy of Kant.

In the latter part of the eighteenth century, Kant's philosophical masterpiece, *Critique of Pure Reason* (1933 [1787]), dealt a severe blow to the confidence of any rationalist theology to establish the existence of God through cognitive means alone. Reason has its limits, and religious belief must operate within the same parameters as every other activity of the human mind. Thus, after Kant, any possible knowledge of the world as constituted and held in being by a loving and benevolent Creator is regarded as impossible, because 'knowledge' is constituted by what the mind itself constructs from the data provided by the senses. God, for Kant, does not fall into this category of things known through the senses and so must be approached in another way. This other way is faith, but faith in the Kantian scheme of things is of purely practical import for ordering our moral lives in response to the universal moral law. It is practical reason which allows us to introduce God, to aid us in our attempts to adhere to the moral law which every rational being can discern independently of religious belief. If one believes in God, then that is simply one's option to view the world from a faith perspective rather than from some other. As Kant put it in uncharacteristically succinct fashion, he had to do away with knowledge in order to make room for faith. The Christian religion, which had been the basis of the worldview of the West – the lens, one could say, through which reality was perceived – now begins to give way to a privatized faith which reflects only the perspective of the individual. Religion is simply an optional standpoint from which to view the world and one's moral responsibility within it.

We have here already the religion of modernity, which is so familiar to us. Here the world becomes the object of our subjective gaze and God, heretofore the origin of *my* being, becomes now dependent on my experience. The world of pre-modernity is inverted and God is now only real if God can be experienced by the individual subject. If I lack such experience then I have no grounds for belief, for God cannot be known cognitively and only some form of religious experience can be the basis of faith. This, the legacy of Kant, presents us with a double bind: no cognitive knowledge of God is possible because such knowledge is outside the limits of the powers of reason; and faith, lacking any rational foundation, is reduced to an optional aspect of a morality established on non-religious grounds.

From the perspective of modernity's emphasis on personal liberty and freedom of conscience, this option to believe or not to believe is undoubtedly considered a positive gain. Freedom of religion is now defended by law in most developed countries and has been enshrined in international human rights agreements. Many Christian churches which once condemned freedom of religion as pernicious now defend the principle, first articulated systematically by John Locke and Pierre Bayle in the seventeenth century, that belief cannot be coerced and that in matters of religion one's conscience is inviolable. Yet the freedom to believe or not to believe did not come without a cost to Christianity, and the primary cost was the separation of the world from the God who had been understood, at least since the time of Saint Augustine in the fifth century, to be the ground of its existence, the source of its value and the goal of its history. The West seemed to have reached the conclusion that when religion does not matter so much any more, it is not difficult to allow everyone freedom to believe whatever they wish.

Reacting to Kant's split between the world and the knowing subject, the thought of Hegel in the early decades of the nineteenth century attempted to put reality back together again through an ambitious and over-reaching project in which the whole of history is encapsulated in the development of 'Mind' (the German term *Geist* can also mean 'Spirit', and has a religious connotation in Hegel's philosophy). Hegel's mature philosophy attempted to lay God to rest through consigning religion to a stage in the developing consciousness of humanity's historical self-awareness, which is to be brought to its apex in philosophy (i.e., in the philosophy of Hegel himself). Indeed, Hegel's philosophy implies that the death of God has already occurred, on the principle that the owl of Minerva always flies at sunset; that is to say, philosophy does not direct the future but comes along at the end of the age to explain the past to the present, an idea inverted by Marx to monumental, but disastrous, effect in his 'Theses on Feuerbach': 'The philosophers have interpreted the world, the point now is to change it' (Marx, 1989 [1845], p. 15).

In the thought of Hegel, human history is the history of the collective Mind coming to its own self-understanding; but this self-understanding is ultimately non-transcendent, for it comes to its zenith in Hegel's own system. Thus the meaning of history is to be found within history itself (again, a view which had a profound influence on Marx). Religion is nothing more than the stage through which history passes on its way to the realization of its own destiny, which has now occurred because Hegel has come along to understand and explain it. Hegel's great insight into the effect of Kant's epistemology was that even if we admitted that God exists independently of our world and our own understanding, God still becomes something unnecessary for the world, which now contains its own internal rationale and is the source of its own value. After Descartes and Kant, the world and the subject are separated. Religious belief, no longer having the status of knowledge, is reduced to an event in the interior world of the individual conscience (which German Pietism was advocating as the true form of Christianity) and the Christian God is thereby dissociated from the world as such.

Later nineteenth-century critiques of theism, such as Ludwig Feuerbach's thesis that God is nothing more than the projection of our deepest aspirations, or Karl Marx's view that religion functions to deflect the attention of the poor from their real economic and social conditions, can be seen as working out this basic Hegelian premise that the meaning of the world is to be found within the world, without any need for a divine Being. Hegel is also the progenitor of panentheism, the view that God is in the world and the world is in God, a position which became an attractive option for theism when the idea of God as a divine being outside the world became problematic (see, for instance, Küng, 1978, pp. 185–8). For Hegel, whose philosophy brought heaven down to earth, the transcendent God of classical Christian thought passed away serenely, no doubt pleased that his work as the progenitor of a more rational philosophy was well spent in the service of a higher purpose. It was left to Nietzsche to see the real cataclysmic impact that the death of God would have for modern consciousness and the culture of the West.

The following passage from Nietzsche's *The Joyful Science* (1882) is the most powerful nineteenth-century text on the death of God. More than any other thinker in that century Nietzsche articulated the spirit of the age and anticipated many of the more significant aspects of modernity and postmodernity. The significance of Nietzsche's prophetic madman lies not, as is commonly thought by his modern and postmodern acolytes, primarily as a progenitor of atheism through the proclamation of the death of God, which Nietzsche was well aware had already occurred in Western culture. Rather, the text is striking for its profound agonizing about the implications of this event for the whole cultural, social and religious fabric of Western society.

Have you not heard of that madman who lit a lantern in the bright morning hours, ran to the market-place and cried incessantly: 'I am looking for God! I am looking for God!' – As many of those who did not believe in God were standing together there he excited considerable laughter . . . The madman sprang into their midst and pierced them with his glances. 'Where has God gone?' he cried. 'I shall tell you. *We have killed him* – you and I. We are all his murderers. But how have we done this? How were we able to drink up the sea? Who gave us the sponge to wipe away the entire horizon? What did we do when we unchained this earth from its sun? Whither is it moving now? Whither are we moving now? Away from all suns? Are we not perpetually falling? Backward, sideward, forward, in all directions? Is there any up or down left? Are we not straying as through an infinite nothing? Do we not feel the breath of empty space? Has it not become colder? Is more and more night not coming on all the time? Must not lanterns be lit in the morning? Do we not hear anything yet of the noise of the gravediggers who are burying God? Do we not smell anything yet of God's decomposition? – gods, too, decompose. God is dead and we have killed him. How shall we, the murder-

ers of all murderers, console ourselves?' . . . – It has been
related further that on that same day the madman
entered divers churches and there sang a *requiem
aeternam deo*. Led out and quieted, he is said to have
retorted each time: 'What are these churches now if they
are not the tombs and sepulchres of God?' (Nietzsche,
1987 [1882], pp. 202–3)

This remarkable passage captures with drama and vivid
imagination what Nietzsche regarded as both the greatness
and the trauma of a culture which was in the process of dis-
pensing with God as the foundation of its values and
self-identity. Like many of his contemporaries, Nietzsche
welcomed the demise of God for the liberation which it would
bring from what he regarded as the stultifying effects of bour-
geois Christian culture and morality. More importantly still,
he perceived what others then and since have not, namely
that no culture could undermine its own foundations without
experiencing a wrenching upheaval which called into
question its own deepest assumptions about itself. This is the
meaning of the vivid and apocalyptic language which Nietzsche places in the mouth of the madman, the new John the
Baptist, who has come too early for his message to be understood. The bystanders who mock the madman, even though
they do not believe in God, fail to understand what they have
done in killing him; their mockery is reduced to astonished
silence, yet the deed is too great for them to comprehend its
gravity and the madman leaves them with the augury that
'deeds, though done, still require time to be seen and heard'.

Nietzsche's virulent anti-Christianity convinced him that
the death of God was such a momentous event that the
churches would become God's tombs and sepulchres, a pre-
diction not too much at variance with the story of the
Christian churches in many Western countries in the nineteenth and twentieth centuries. Yet the principal import of

his insights is not the reduction in church attendance, but the way in which we find meaning and purpose in a culture which has come into existence imbued with the spirit of Christianity and must now cope without the source from which its creativity flowed. Only when we view the death of God with Nietzsche not merely as an event to be celebrated – as secular Western culture has done and continues to do – but also as a disconnection from our origins which we have not yet learned to comprehend, only then will we be in a position to begin to deal with the disorientation and perplexity which mark our attempts to understand our own times. Despite its many achievements, the failure of secular culture to keep both poles of Nietzsche's dialectic together – both the sense of liberation and the sense of dislocation – is the root of our postmodern bafflement. With Nietzsche, can we not all feel that the world has grown colder without God?

Viewed from this perspective, the attempts of nineteenth- and twentieth-century art, music and literature to find secular redemption in high culture was only a hiatus before the full import of the death of God was extended to other dimensions of our worlds of meaning. The vision of a redemptive modernist culture, as articulated above all by Matthew Arnold and brought to expression in Gauguin and Cézanne, in Joyce and Proust, in Schoenberg and Picasso, was a truly valiant attempt within Western culture to replace the religious with an aesthetic transcendence. In the best of modernist culture we find the urge to articulate the transcendent through the ordinary – a day in Dublin in which a whole lifetime of experience is encapsulated, the world evoked by the taste of a small madeleine, the glories of a bowl of fruit which will make the viewer see every subsequent piece of fruit differently, or the musical tones which provoke the ear into experiencing listening in a new way.

Many of the great modernist artists in the first half of the twentieth century sought to replace the divine with the sublime and at the same time to resist the levelling of culture which the mass-production techniques of industrial capitalism brought (the very same levelling which is celebrated by postmodernism). But the inexorable logic of the death of God attests that this attempt was ill-fated from the beginning, for when God is done away with we cannot continue as before; when the origin of value is extinguished, all values are transformed. From this perspective the mid-twentieth-century agonizing of existentialism (in the pessimism of Sartre, Camus and Beckett) as well as the parodying within modernism of modernism's own highest aspirations (in Dadaism, Surrealism and the Theatre of the Absurd) may be regarded both as an attempt to forestall the inevitable degradation of culture and also an anticipation of the postmodern context in which we now live. In our contemporary context, however, stimulated beyond measure by the disposable icons of consumerism, we seem to have suppressed the agony of our loss while replacing the real with its own ersatz parody: the shopping mall for the cathedral, the psychoanalyst for the confessor, the rock star for the saint, and the ego for the soul. But is it not the case that the fetishization of the needful self in capitalist culture serves only to repress our recognition of the enormity of our deed?

Despite his antipathy towards Christianity, it was Nietzsche's greatness (and, for the most part, his followers' failure) that he first perceived that the death of God would result in the death of many other sacred elements also. This is beautifully expressed by Leszek Kolakowski:

Even atheists, Nietzsche among them, knew this: order and meaning come from God, and if God really is dead, then we delude ourselves in thinking meaning can be saved. If God is dead nothing remains but an indifferent void which engulfs and annihilates us. No trace remains of our lives and our labours; there is only the meaningless dance of protons and electrons. The universe wants nothing and cares for nothing; it strives towards no goal; it neither rewards nor punishes. Whoever says that there is no God and all is well deceives himself. (Kolakowski, 1999, pp. 116–17)

Notwithstanding the hiatus of high-modernity's attempts to find solace for the absence of God in the aesthetic, postmodernity has fulfilled Nietzsche's prophecy. It accomplished this in Western culture by gleefully killing off other sacred icons: the death of the author and the novel (Roland Barthes), the death of 'man' (Michel Foucault), the death of narrative and history (Jean-François Lyotard), the death of the sign and the written word (Jacques Derrida) have all been proclaimed as great liberating discoveries of our age, but are in truth little more than a series of footnotes to Nietzsche.

Perhaps the great dereliction of both modernity and postmodernity is their failure to comprehend fully the immense impact which the death of God in the culture of the West has had on our sense of ourselves, and consequently on the possibility of retrieving a meaning or meanings which can return us to ourselves. Not that we can ever recreate what some like to think of as the seamless garment of premodernity; even if such a golden era had ever existed, which is improbable, it would be neither desirable nor possible to attempt to recreate it. Those who take the opportunity of our postmodern condition to rejoice in the failure of secular modernity to offer the equivalent cultural coherence which religion once did, should take no satisfaction from our current predicament. Reactionary attempts to recreate the past succeed only in making the present more unbearable, and there is no way around either modernity or postmodernity, only through them. We can no more recreate the past of a harmonious Christian culture than we can return the *ancien régime* to France or the rule of monarchy to the USA.

When, with Hegel and Nietzsche, we think of the death of God as a cultural event of enormous consequence, an event whose significance we are incapable of grasping fully, then we realize too that the death of God has little or nothing to do with God (for if God is God, then God as such cannot die) and everything to do with us, with our estimation of ourselves, with our understanding of our identity and sense of purpose, with our hopes for our culture and our history. If the death of God is the death of all that is founded on God, then the death of God may leave us in despair for all that we hold dear, and it is the recognition of this despair which modernity in its various guises attempted to defer. But when postmodernity took the mask off the great attempts of modernity to replace God with the pseudo-scientific mythologies of Marxism, Freudianism, Fascism, Existentialism, Socialism and Capitalism, or even with the redemptive power of art, we were left alone with ourselves. How do we then seek consolation? By becoming gods ourselves, as Nietzsche advocated? Hardly. The twentieth century's political attempts at this aggrandizement have been ruinous. And today, with the populations of the capitalist cultures of the West held in slavery by the myth of unlimited growth and consumption, the modernist attempts to achieve the apotheosis of the self look like a child's dream that became a nightmare.

Writing in the middle of the nineteenth century, Søren Kierkegaard equated our modern condition with bewilderment and despair, which he regarded as essentially the same thing. Like that other great analyst of our misery, Blaise Pascal, Kierkegaard perceived the ills of modernity before they became apparent to others. Despair, says Kierkegaard, is the condition of the modern individual, the 'sickness in the self' which leaves us disoriented yet mostly unaware of the source of our own malaise. Despair *is* the sickness unto death, where the *unto* refers to the fact that we cannot die to rid ourselves of our despair. Contrary to Camus 100 years later, Kierkegaard knows that we must live with despair, for this does not ultimately concern the death of the body but the dying of the self: 'To be delivered from the sickness of death is an impossibility, for the sickness and its torment – and death – consist in not being able to die' (Kierkegaard, 1946 [1849], p. 344). The dying of the self is the dying of the possibility of meaning, of value and of truth. But it does not have to be this way, for we can choose to recognize that being a self is 'the greatest concession made to man, but at the same time it is eternity's demand on him' (Kierkegaard 1946 [1849], p. 344).

But to be a true 'self' after the death of God: is that not to demand the impossible? Are not all 'selves' now undone? The fear of despair in the face of the bewildering remnant of the self after the death of God – one of the distinguishing marks of the modern – was the impulse behind the project of twenti-eth-century existentialism to challenge each person to take responsibility for their own self-creation. Camus missed an opportunity for greatness when he said that the only real question for his time and generation was the question of suicide, for Kierkegaard had already seen through this evasion.

As Kierkegaard realized, the real question is: what could it mean to be a self if there is no God? The final exit of suicide is not the answer to the question of meaninglessness in a world without God, for it only evades the problem. Nor, contrary to many of his philosophical retinue in the twentieth century, did Kierkegaard believe that we could resolve our dilemma either through an act of self-creation as ethical beings, or through that other path of modernist redemption, the aes-thetic. For him only the religious answer is a final answer. But in a culture such as ours, is this a real possibility; is the leap of faith a realistic option to return us to ourselves?

The widespread religious response to the challenge of modernity and postmodernity is the conviction that a return to God can restore the fragments of our culture to a lost unity (this I perceive to be the point of Pope John Paul's well-known aspiration for a Christian Europe from the Atlantic to the Urals). But if what we have said about the death of God is true, then before the return of God becomes even thinkable we must know and understand more about our own condition. To know our situation and to understand it: this was the message of both Pascal and Kierkegaard, and it remains the only avenue open to a culture after the death of God. Rediscover God and the self will follow, may be the logical theological step, but it is not the path of cultural redemption. We must first understand ourselves and the deprivation as experienced by a culture which has attempted to live without its own deepest grounds.

If, with Nietzsche, we can see that the death of God is an event which happens more to us than to God, we can then perceive that the death of God is the symptom, not the cause, of our own despair. For this reason, a nostalgic return to some golden age of religion, so desired by many religious believers in a state of gloom at our present condition, is not the answer to our predicament; masking the symptom does not cure the illness. It is too much to expect that a return of God can cure us of the despair of which the death of God in our culture is but a feature. Modern atheism believes, with Feuerbach, that God is nothing more than the projection of our desires onto an eternal and all-powerful Being; but, turning Feuerbach against himself, we could equally argue that the death of God in our culture is nothing more than the projection onto God of our own hopelessness. If this is the case – and, we must emphasize, it is not a question of fact but a question of perception and discernment – then modern atheism is a curious phenomenon. Ostensibly a liberation from God, it abandons us to the perilous state of being saviours to ourselves. From Kant to Marx to Nietzsche to Sartre and Beckett, the modernist move away from God was always paralleled by the demand that the human person bears the weight of selfhood, morality, history and law on herself. Postmodernism, with its unravelling of all identities, is but the realization that this burden is impossible for the self to bear. If God is dead in our culture, then we all – believer and unbeliever alike – must live with the consequences of that loss.

3

On Not Knowing God

Now pay attention: God is nameless, because no one can say anything or understand anything about him. (Meister Eckhart, *German Sermons*, 1981, n. 83)

God is in heaven, and you upon earth; therefore let your words be few. (Ecclesiastes 5.2)

Judaism bequeathed to Christianity not only a rich storehouse of specific metaphors for God, but also a tradition that Yahweh was ultimately a mystery which the human mind could not comprehend. Inheriting this legacy, early Christian thinkers faced their own set of problems in thinking about God. For them there was no question of God being absent from or incapable of intervening in history, as their belief was that God had acted decisively on behalf of all humanity in the life, death and resurrection of Jesus Christ, and continued to live with the Church in the person of the Holy Spirit. From its Jewish heritage, Christianity received a substantially, although not exclusively, anthropomorphic idea of God from which it developed its own specific theology of God's saving action in the person of Jesus Christ and in the ongoing presence of the Holy Spirit.

When Christianity encountered the Hellenistic world it began to draw on concepts from Greek philosophy to further develop its idea of God. From the emphasis which Greek

thought places on the notion of *being*, Christian theology
began to think of God in philosophical terms as the highest
conceivable Being, qualitatively and not simply quantitat-
ively different from other beings. In the Greek philosophical
tradition God was thought of in terms of substance or sub-
stantiality, with certain attributes and characteristics
particular to God's being. But God in this view was in no way
external to nature; God was part of nature and therefore
subject to its unalterable laws. When Greek pagan critics of
Christianity, such as Galen, considered the Christians' idea of
God, they were shocked at what they regarded as its philosophical inadequacy. In the words of Robert Wilken, the
Creator God of the Christians seemed to pagans to be 'a
capricious and unbridled deity who brought the world into
being by an act of will without reference to his actions' (1984,
p. 86).

Faced with this form of criticism, Christians attempted to
demonstrate to pagans that they too worshipped the one high
God of the Greeks, and not simply the man Jesus crucified in
Palestine. The result was an attempt to bring together the
Jewish and Christian idea of God with that of the Greeks. The
conjunction of Jewish and Christian anthropomorphism with
Greek notions of being and of identity as substance produced
the idea of God as a Super-Being, a real yet totally transcendent personality, capable of acting in history and influencing
the lives of ordinary people in extraordinary ways.

When these two emphases – the Jewish anthropomorphic
emphasis and the Greek philosophical emphasis – came
together in Christian theology, there began to emerge a more
reified (from the Latin *res*, 'thing') notion of God which objectified the notion of God as a Being above all other beings
(Kaufman, 1996, p. 147). Even when God was thought of as
triune – in liturgy, prayer or doctrine – there was usually also
present the distinct image of God's unity as a single Being.
This has left us with a heritage in Western theology and

philosophy in which it is almost a given to think of God as one, as personal, and as transcendent. The popular images of God as a Being separate from the world which this theological and philosophical tradition helped form are very familiar to us, but this tradition has also left us with a strong imagery about the separation of God and the world which at times takes on a dualistic aspect: God is God, and God is 'up' or 'out' there for all eternity; we are sinful humans and we are 'down' here, strutting our hour upon this passing stage.

However, as well as this influential tradition which emphasized the notion of God as a powerful, transcendent, perfect, and yet personal Being, there also developed a more mystical tradition in which the incomprehensibility of God as total mystery was emphasized. As Gordon Kaufman points out, while most Western thinkers have found it difficult to think of God in terms other than a particular mode of being or substance, another strand of the theological tradition, namely the mystical strand, has laid a somewhat different stress on the notion of God as ultimately unknowable:

> Only in the mystical tradition was the idea seriously entertained that the difference between God and particular beings might be better expressed by moving in precisely the opposite direction. That is, by interpreting the divine as not-existing, as radical non-being, instead of interpreting it positively in terms of the notion of being. (1996, p. 148)

In this chapter I want to look at some representative figures and ideas from that mystical tradition and relate these to some of our contemporary concerns about the idea of God. We will see that the questions about God raised by our modern world have some parallel aspects to questions raised in other eras, although the way in which we formulate our answers will be different.

In the Christian disputes about the doctrine of the Trinity which marked the fourth century of the Common Era, not only the theological exposition of the Christian notion of God was at issue, but also the very question about what human beings could say at all about the divine reality. While the major ecumenical councils of the Church were attempting to lay down doctrinal definitions which would satisfy the Christian experience of God and provide a unified belief system for the Roman Empire, some theologians were thinking of the question of the capacity of human thought to reach out to the mystery of the divine nature. The most important of these thinkers were the Cappadocians (from eastern Turkey): Basil of Caesarea (329–79), his brother Gregory of Nyssa (335–95), and their friend Gregory Nazianzus (329–91).

For the Cappadocians, human minds could never expect to grasp the essence of the ineffable God and an apophatic approach (i.e. speaking of something through negation) was considered essential to Christian theological reflection. However, it was also important for these thinkers – as leaders of a living community of Christians – not to neglect a cataphatic approach (speaking through affirmation). Thus, the question of how to balance the Christian community's unavoidable talk of God in its prayer, liturgy and doctrine with a denial of the capacity of that talk to ever achieve knowledge of the being of God, was central to the way these influential early theologians perceived the task of Christian theology.

The Cappadocians, like most Christians, thought of God as an individual, transcendent Being who exists outside the world yet who is also capable of personal interaction with his creatures. If God had chosen to be revealed to humans, then we must be capable, in some way or other, of understanding something about God as God. The challenge for theology then, as they saw it, was to explain how the weakness of the human mind could grasp in any way the transcendent reality of this infinite and ineffable God, who despite his majesty had made us in his image and likeness. For them, the answer to this problem was that any assumption of final understanding of God had to be resisted, and for this to be realized a negative approach to talking about God was constitutive of their theology. For the Cappadocians, as Jaroslav Pelikan puts it, '[n]egative theology was indispensable, because resorting to either language or thought in hopes of comprehending the Incomprehensible was like playing a children's game and deluding oneself that the fantasy was for real' (1993, p. 42).

In his *Life of Moses*, Gregory of Nyssa comments on Moses' approach to the cloud in which God was hidden (Exodus 20.21) in order to make the point that it is in not knowing that we truly know:

> The mind leaves behind all that appears, not only what the senses grasp, but also whatever the intelligence seems to behold and ever seeks to move further inward, until it penetrates by reason of the activity of the intelligence to what is unseen and incomprehensible and there sees God. *For it is precisely in this that true knowledge of what is sought consists, that is in not seeing, because we seek what lies beyond all knowledge,* shrouded by incomprehensibility in all directions, as it were by some cloud. (Gregory of Nyssa, 1999, 2.163, trans. Anthony Meredith [emphasis mine])

We may approach God, we may attempt to understand, but the closer we get to what we think is understanding, the deeper in the cloud of incomprehensibility we find ourselves. Like Moses, as we seem to increase in knowledge of God, this only enables us to grasp that the divine is ineffable, 'above all knowledge and comprehension' (Gregory of Nyssa, 1999, 2.164). In knowing, we come to know that we do not know.

Basil of Caesarea, the brother of Gregory of Nyssa, was acutely sensitive to the danger of the orthodox theologian being trapped in epistemological scepticism about knowledge of God. The danger was that those hostile to Christianity would take the refusal to speak of the nature of God as an admission of complete ignorance. Basil was well aware of the conundrum:

> [People ask,] 'Do you worship what you know or what you do not know?' If I answer 'I worship what I know', they immediately reply, 'What is the essence of the object of worship?' Then, if I confess that I am ignorant of the essence, they turn on me again and say, 'So, you worship you know not what!' I answer that the word 'to know' has many meanings. We say that we know the greatness of God, the power of God, the wisdom of God, the goodness of God, the providence of God over us, and the justness of the judgment of God, but not the very *ousia* [being] of God. (Basil of Caesarea, in Pelikan, 1993, p. 55)

The Cappadocians steadfastly refused to admit that human words about God ever reached to the *ousia* of God, maintaining that this was not revealed to us because it was not necessary for our salvation. But what was revealed to us were the names of God such as the imagery employed in the scriptures or the qualities of God described by philosophers. The human mind, limited as it is, requires such names, even though God in God's own being does not.

Basil's problem in trying to speak of God yet also defend the idea that God is unknowable is fairly typical of the sort of problem which Christian theology produces when it wants to talk of a transcendent, infinite, ineffable Being who is also capable of being known to some extent by the human mind. Basil's solution, namely to distinguish between the attributes of God which we can know and the true being of God which we cannot know, was to become a common Christian answer to this dilemma. We know as much as God has chosen to reveal to us for our salvation, and no more. The prominence given to the unknowability of the being of God, even though it is still operating with a reified concept of God, opened up the possibility of talking about God as ultimately incomprehensible, and provided a balance within Christian theology to the emphasis which the Church placed on the positive knowledge of the revealed truths deemed necessary for salvation. Furthermore, rather than being a defeat for the human mind, this inability to understand God could be understood as enhancing human freedom: Jaroslav Pelikan makes the important point that

> negative theology could be construed not only as a limitation on the mind but at the same time as a liberation of the mind, setting the human reason, as the image of God, free to pursue its speculations within the boundaries which had been set for it. (1993, p. 57)

In other words, the human mind has an appropriate domain of knowledge which it is free to investigate, but knowledge of the divine nature is not within that realm. Thus, in some respects the weakness of the human mind enables the freedom of reason within its proper boundaries. (In a later Christian context – that of Protestantism – the idea of the utter majesty of God's transcendence over the mundane world, so leaving the human being free to work within the temporal realm, had a significant influence on the development of the modern Western consciousness.)

Later Christian tradition took the notion of the incomprehensibility of God even further. The fifth- or sixth-century author known as Pseudo-Dionysius placed the theological emphasis less on the limitations of the human mind and more on the incomprehensibility of the divine nature.

Pseudo-Dionysius tried to hold in tension the apparently paradoxical ideas that God is revealed in the whole of the creation and in the specific Christian revelation while at the same time retaining the idea that God is totally unknowable. He did this by drawing on the neo-Platonic view that there is an outpouring of the divine nature into the created reality, and that from this divine self-expression some positive knowledge may be gleaned. However, this positive outpouring is countered, or negated, by the return of all things into the ineffable divine nature.

Thus, in his *The Divine Names*, Pseudo-Dionysius can give a wholly philosophical account of God's impassible nature as Supreme Being

> God is transcendently, eternally, unalterably, and invariably the 'same'. He is forever thus . . . located within the fine boundaries of his own supra-essential identity. In him there is no change, decline, deterioration or variation. He is unalloyed, immaterial, totally simple, self-sufficient, subject to neither growth nor diminution . . . (1987, 9, 4)

This is the transcendent God as pure Being, containing all perfections within the divine nature. In his *Symbolic Theology* (now lost) Pseudo-Dionysius deals with the more anthropomorphic ideas of God, and in the *Mystical Theology* he gives a short summary of this treatment:

> I have spoken of his [God's] anger, grief and rage, of how he is said to be drunk and hung-over, of his oaths and curses, of his sleeping and waking, and indeed of all those images we have of him, images shaped by the workings of the symbolic representations of God. (1987, Chapter 3)

This is the anthropomorphic God familiar to us from the Bible and from Christian piety, yet it is the same God as the God of all the perfections listed in *The Divine Names*; it is simply God known in another way, this time symbolically rather than conceptually.

However, both the symbolic and the conceptual must give way when the mind begins to understand all things as returning to the ineffable God. Everything changes for Pseudo-Dionysius when we attempt to go beyond that which can be known by the intellect:

> ... now as we plunge into that darkness which is beyond intellect, we shall find ourselves not simply running short of words but actually speechless and unknowing ... and the more it climbs the more language falters, and when it has passed up and beyond the ascent, it will turn silent completely, since it will finally be at one with him who is indescribable. (1987, Chapter 3)

All theology, all talk of God, comes to an end in silence which acknowledges that God is beyond anything which human beings could possibly say:

> [God or 'the Cause of all'] 'cannot be spoken of and cannot be grasped by understanding ... It has no power, it is not power, nor is it light. It does not live nor is it life. It is not a substance, nor is it eternity or time. It cannot be grasped by the understanding since it is neither knowledge nor truth. It is not kingship. It is not wisdom. It is neither one nor oneness, divinity nor goodness ... It falls neither within the predicate of non-being nor of being. Existing beings do not know it as it actually is and it does not know them as they are ... It is beyond assertion and denial. (1987, Chapter 5)

God is unknown and unknowable, infinitely beyond both being and non-being and, in our contemporary expression, beyond both theism and atheism.

In order to appreciate just how radical is this view of 'the Cause of all' (which Pseudo-Dionysius does not at this point call 'God') we have to emphasize that our negating the positive ideas and images of God – both the anthropomorphic, symbolic ones and the conceptual, philosophical ones – does not result in us somehow mystically conceptualizing or comprehending the divine nature (which in any case is beyond words like 'divinity') as simply a negation of the positive descriptors of the cataphatic theology; Pseudo-Dionysius makes it clear that our negations too must be negated until we end in silence. Thus the view recently expressed by Francis Schüssler Fiorenza and Gordon D. Kaufman that *The Divine Names* and the *Mystical Theology* 'affirm that one can only posit negative statements about God' is not strictly correct (see Fiorenza and Kaufman, 1998, p. 150), for in the words of Pseudo-Dionysius which I have just quoted, the negations are not posited of God but are themselves negated, and this is indicative of our inability to say anything final, either positive or negative, about the being of God.

This radical view of the limitations of all our talk about God had a significant influence on the subsequent mystical and even mainstream theological tradition, although its radical nature was often somewhat attenuated. Thomas Aquinas is an important example of a major theologian who took from Pseudo-Dionysius the idea of God as beyond all affirmation (although he did not insist that God is beyond all negation too):

Now the mode of supereminence in which the . . . perfections are found in God can be signified by names used by us only through negation, as when we say that God is

eternal or *infinite*, or also through a relation of God to
other things, as when He is called the *first cause* or
highest good. For we cannot grasp what God is, but only
what he is not and how other things are related to Him
... (Aquinas, 1955, 1/30.4)

In the first part of the *Summa Theologiae*, in discussing the
question of the existence of God he argues that we must
consider 'how God is not rather than how God is' (*Summa
Theologiae* 1/1, Question 3).

The medieval German mystic, Meister Eckhart
(1260–1327), developed the *via negativa* in terms of a
theology and spirituality which focused on the union of the
soul with God. Eckhart's thought is complex, and is heavily
influenced by neo-Platonism, but his spirituality is profound
and daring, and even tends towards pantheism in its
emphasis on the union of God with the soul of the believer.
Particularly in the sermons delivered in his native German,
Eckhart seeks to explain his understanding of the manner in
which God can be understood as indwelling in the soul. It is a
recurring theme of Eckhart's that in the life of the Trinity,
God the Father gives birth to God the Son in a movement in
which God is fecund, even 'verdant and growing with all his
divinity'. In a similar way the outflowing of the divine nature
can enable God to come to birth in the soul of the Christian so
that the soul is infused with the divine presence. God's
presence in the soul comes to be by means of a principle or
element of the soul to which Eckhart gives various names. In
the second German sermon he calls it 'a light of the spirit'
(Eckhart, 1981, p. 180) but he also gives it other names such
as 'ground', 'intellect' and 'spark'. These are attempts to name
the unnameable, to grasp how God can be known as present:

[Y]et whatever fine names, whatever words we use, they
are telling lies, and it is far above them. It is free of all

names, it is bare of all forms, wholly empty and free, as God in himself is empty and free. (Eckhart, 1981, p. 180)

This presence or 'birth' of God in the soul of the believer becomes for Eckhart the heart of the religious experience. Yet he sometimes speaks as though there is no difference between God and the innermost depths of the self: 'If my life is God's being, then God's existence must be my existence and God's is-ness is my is-ness, neither less nor more' (Eckhart, 1981, p. 187). In the mystical union of the soul with God the divisions are blurred and the soul merges with God, and God with the soul. But what are we to make of this daring suggestion? Is Eckhart suggesting that God is nothing more than the highest principle of the soul? The answer to this question will probably always elude us; as Denys Turner puts it in his book, *The Darkness of God: Negativity in Christian Mysticism*: 'It is notoriously difficult to say how near Eckhart's hyperbolic language drives him to a pantheistic form of identification of the "ground of God" with the "ground of the soul"' (1995, p. 141). But, while Eckhart goes further than most in his stress on the union of God and soul, we should not lose sight of the fact, as Turner warns us, that '[s]ome version of the soul's ultimate identity with God is the common stock in trade of the whole Western mystical tradition, at least until as late as the sixteenth century' (p. 143).

So, while most Eckhart scholars deny that Eckhart thought that God was nothing more than the human raised to its highest potential (see, for example, Davies, 1991, p. xxvi), at the very least Eckhart is open to various interpretations. In his attempt to emphasize the radical immanence of the presence of God in the human heart, he tended to downplay the transcendence of God and was, in his own lifetime, suspected of pantheism. This is conceivable when one also sees the radical manner in which he thought of God's own being, for Eckhart was disposed to speak of the unity of

God much more than of God as Trinity, and he thought of that
unity as beyond all prevailing forms of knowledge and understanding other than that available to the soul alone. Like
many of the mystics he wanted to speak of the Godhead
which dwelt beyond all concepts and formulations of the
divine, including those of the most sacred doctrinal formulations.

In his German sermon No. 48 he speaks as though the
Christian trinitarian doctrine was secondary, if not irrele-
vant, to the pure, inaccessible, divine nature which the soul
can encounter:

> That is why I say that if a man will turn away from
> himself and from all created things, by so much will you
> be made one and blessed in the spark in the soul . . . This
> spark rejects all created things, and wants nothing but
> its naked God as he is in himself. It is not content with
> the Father or the Son or the Holy Spirit . . . [and] it wants
> to go into the simple ground, into the quiet desert, into
> which distinction never gazed, not the Father, nor the
> Son, nor the Holy Spirit. (Eckhart, 1981, p. 198).

The pure, simple, unity of the Godhead is beyond all categories and beyond all description; it may be experienced in
the sublime spiritual experience, but it can never be comprehended as such or spoken of with certitude: 'We cannot find a
single name we might give to God' (Eckhart, 1981, p. 204). Yet
paradoxically, when the soul abandons the attempt to think
of God in concepts or images, it can encounter the true God:

> Even if the soul contemplates God, either as God or as an
> image or as three, the soul lacks something. But if all
> images are detached from the soul, and it contemplates
> only the Simple One, then the soul's naked being finds
> the naked, formless being of the divine unity. . . . Ah,

marvel of marvels, how noble is that acceptance, when the soul's being can accept nothing else than the naked unity of God! (Eckhart, 1981, p. 206)

While it is unlikely that Eckhart intended to stray outside the lines of orthodoxy, these passages indicate that he was, however, prepared to push the conceptual theological boundaries to their imaginative limits. In thinking of the Godhead as beyond all concepts, as totally ineffable, Eckhart placed it beyond all doctrine and dogma. In emphasizing the intimate, 'naked' union of the soul with the divine 'Simple One' he made the intensity of the religious experience primary and brought the transcendence of God into the immanence of the human heart. It would be an unjustified anachronism to infer from this that Eckhart intended to reduce God to human religious experience – he was not a modern in that sense – but he did, nonetheless, open the possibilities for later thinking to do just that. This, perhaps, partly accounts for his popularity today.

After Eckhart, the *via negativa* had one further great medieval advocate, the fifteenth-century Cardinal, Nicholas of Cusa. In his *Dialogue on the Hidden God (Dialogus de deo abscondito)* (1444), Cusa develops the idea of our human condition of 'ignorance', which he had set out more systematically in his earlier *magnum opus, Of Learned Ignorance (De docta ignorantia)* (1440).

In the earlier work, Cusa had spoken of the ignorance which knows that it is ignorance, and like Socrates before him, he realizes that knowing he is ignorant in fact makes him wise; that is, he is 'learned' and 'ignorant' at the same time. What he is ignorant of, above all, is God's true nature. While Christians require positive images and words for God in order to worship God and to know God as triune, as wise, as good and so on, knowledge of God can be attained more truly through learned ignorance. The 'darkness of our ignorance' cannot comprehend the light of the divine nature, and so all affirmative theology requires a negative theology also; otherwise 'God would not be worshipped as the infinite God but as creature; and such worship is idolatry, for it gives to an image that which belongs only to truth itself.' We note that Cusa has included the doctrine of the Trinity in what belongs to positive theology and he goes on to press home the point that when we consider the divine nature from the perspective of infinity, 'nothing other than infinity is found in God. Consequently, negative theology holds that God is unknowable either in this world or in the world to come . . .' (*Of Learned Ignorance*, 1997, pp. 126–7). As he has already said that learned ignorance is superior to the knowledge of God expressed in the positive affirmations of Christian worship, the final conclusion is that God is revealed to us as incomprehensible.

This theme is taken even further in the *Dialogue on the Hidden God*. There, a Christian is quizzed by a pagan on his notion of God. Each time the pagan seeks to gain some definition or positive image of God, the Christian refuses to acknowledge that God can be known. When the pagan asks how he can worship what he does not know, the Christian replies that he worships *because* he does not know. When the pagan construes the Christian's view of God as being nothing, the Christian replies that God is not 'nothing', but nor is God 'something': 'God is neither nothing nor not nothing, nor is God both nothing and not nothing, but God is the source and origin of all beginnings of being and not-being.' But when the pagan seems to agree that God is the origin of being and not-being the Christian asserts that God is not that. The pagan points out that this is just what the Christian has said and gets the following reply: 'I was speaking the truth when I said it, and I am speaking the truth now when I deny it. For if there are any beginnings of being and not-being, God comes before them' (*Dialogue on the Hidden God*, 1997, p. 212).

What are we to make of this paradoxical and even bewildering way of thinking of God, which seems so reminiscent of some of the deeper Buddhist paradoxes on the nature of being and non-being? The God who is discussed in Cusa's *Dialogue* seems very distant from the God who is worshipped in the Christian liturgy, prayed to in time of trouble or blessed in time of happiness; this ineffable (and yet, according to Cusa, not ineffable) God seems to be beyond all language, all images and all concepts, and consequently alien to any human approach. Yet Cusa does not see it like this; in his understanding of reality it is possible for opposites to come together in a harmonious unity in which the disparate elements can coexist without being in conflict or without being reduced one to the other. He calls this meeting without conflict or reduction a 'coincidence of opposites' (*coincidentia oppositorum*). It is not our primary concern here to discover whether this is a viable or even coherent idea, except to say that without some such mechanism to resolve the paradox between the positive and the negative theologies, it would be difficult to preserve any connection between the God worshipped in the churches and the austere concept of God given us by the *via negativa*; the path of negation can at times seem to sever the ineffable God from the God of Christian worship and piety. If the apophatic and the cataphatic cannot be brought back together, reconciled so that the God who is hidden is also the God who is worshipped, then the very possibility of having a coherent image of the Christian God becomes problematic.

Modern, post-Enlightenment thinking on this question has had to deal with something more than the theological problem of how the human mind can know anything about the ineffable God; it has also had to come to terms with the epistemological critique which asserts that it is not possible for reason to reach out beyond the boundaries of its own experience to encounter realities which by traditional definition lie outside our world. In our own context, Western thinking about God has had at least 200 years (since Kant) to come to terms with the Enlightenment's critique of knowledge. The most obvious impact of this critique has been that theologians, in terms of God's relation to the self, have focused their efforts on an analysis of religious experience and, in terms of God's relation to the world, have turned towards the option of panentheism (the view which attempts to link God and the world without reducing one to the other, seeing God in the world and the world in God) to explain how God can be both transcendent to the world yet active in it.

The Enlightenment critique of knowledge and the more recent critique of metaphysics associated with Nietzsche, Heidegger and postmodernists such as Jacques Derrida, have both caused immense difficulties for the traditional image of God. Rather than the ancient and medieval question of how the ineffable God may be known by the mind of a sinful creature, the modern and postmodern question is twofold: one is Kant's question of how can reason have knowledge of something beyond itself, and the second is how an ineffable, transcendent, infinite Being can also be thought of as personal. Both of these questions, taken together, have seemed to some to leave contemporary theism in an epistemological and metaphysical cul-de-sac.

One influential form of modern negative theology which has tried to deal with this problem is that associated with the German–American theologian Paul Tillich (1886–1965). Tillich took the view that, rather than thinking of God as the highest being, '[m]any confusions in the doctrine of God and many apologetic weaknesses could be avoided if God were understood first of all as being-itself or as the ground of being' (Tillich, 1984 [1951], p. 235). Like many theologians influenced by the critiques of epistemology and metaphysics, and by the development of modern biblical criticism, Tillich was attracted by an apophatic approach to God. This led him to speak of 'God above the God of theism' (Tillich, 1979 [1952], p. 183), by which he meant the idea of God other than that which is given to us when we think of God as a Being, no matter how elevated we make God when we think of God in this way. Tillich contends that religion is not some separate sphere of human activity, but rather the experience of depth in all our human endeavours, and that God (the highest point of our religious thought) can be thought of as humanity's Ultimate Concern (Tillich, 1984 [1951], pp. 220–3 and *passim*). Thus we can think of God as that which we experience in the very depths of our humanity, without ever thinking that we have conceptually or cognitively grasped that reality fully.

As the title of Tillich's short masterpiece, *The Courage To Be*, indicates, this understanding of God is no mysticism which flies from the world, but the basis of our courage to live and to act in the world. There are notable advantages to thinking of God in this way. The epistemological critique is accepted and so we no longer have to explain how we can have knowledge of a realm beyond experience. The metaphysical critique is answered (to some extent) by thinking of God not as a Being, but as Being-itself, the ground of all that is. However, the price to be paid for this modern form of the *via negativa* is that the transcendence of the traditional God of theism (that is, God as a Being) is more or less abandoned or at least removed to the realm of agnosticism. Then, the problem remains – as it does for all negative theologies – as to how this apophatic view of God is to be related to the positive symbolic, liturgical and doctrinal Christianity which relies so heavily on the positive, cataphatic images and concepts of God. Given the radical *via negativa* which Tillich espoused, we can see why he was suspected of atheism by some of his contemporaries and why his views greatly influenced the death-of-God movement in the twentieth century as well as contemporary non-realist theologies.

In a recent work of philosophical theology, which is likely to influence this discussion for many years, Philip Clayton has been severely critical of Tillich's position, arguing that his 'doctrine of God is not ultimately successful in making the transition from negative to positive theology' (Clayton, 2000, p. 470). The root of Clayton's criticism is that Tillich has too readily accepted the Kantian critique of reason's powers. Tillich had argued in volume one of his *Systematic Theology* that our experience of human finitude opens us to the possibility of the infinite, and that infinity thus 'directs the mind to experience its own unlimited potentialities, but it does not establish the existence of an infinite being' (Tillich, 1979 [1952], p. 190). In other words, he can only accept God as a regulating concept which acts as a focus for our own potentiality, but he cannot move from that position to posit knowledge of an actually existing being. This latter step, for Tillich, is precluded by the rigour of the Kantian epistemological critique.

Furthermore, Clayton is critical of what he perceives as Tillich's misunderstanding of the nature of symbolic language. When Tillich introduces Christian language into his discussion of the human predicament, thinks Clayton, he is not answering any existential or metaphysical questions as the theological language is used as 'purely symbolic' (Clayton, 2000, p. 470). Since we are now no longer so naïve about distinctions between which forms of language are 'symbolic' and which are not, as we now know that *all* language is symbolic, we are free to debate which metaphors for God are more or less adequate. This enables us, in Clayton's view, to 'move beyond the "what God is not" debate, and thus beyond negative theology, in order to reflect on the adequacy and inadequacy of specific types of language about the divine' (2000, p. 471).

There is much more to Clayton's overall project than these points I have highlighted, but with regard to the issue we are considering here, it is difficult to see how recognizing all language as symbolic moves us in any way 'beyond' negative theology. If anything, it moves us 'back' into the pre-Kantian traditional negative theology which was careful to demarcate the cataphatic positive language about God – always understood as symbolic – from the apophatic silence which recognizes the failure of all language to grasp the divine. But if we want to move forward from *there*, then we are simply back where we started in modernity, with all the hermeneutical and theological questions which have engaged us for the past 200 or so years. Without introducing some other external regulating concept, such as a doctrine of authority or a principle drawn from specific revelation which would provide a regulating criterion, it seems to me that Clayton could not achieve a theological adjudication between different symbols or metaphors for God at all, other than on the pragmatic grounds of how they function for particular eras or cultures, or perhaps on ethical grounds. But if we do introduce an external regulating concept, we can no longer claim to be achieving something in the realm of philosophical theology, but would be engaged in a form of dogmatic theology based on an external authority.

Like the traditional advocates of the *via negativa* who had to treat *all* the metaphors for God as equally adequate and equally inadequate because they were all part of the inspired Holy Scripture, Clayton's position – without some external rule to enable us to judge – returns us to a point where all metaphors are equal because all language is equally symbolic. This is just the situation faced by Pseudo-Dionysius, Eckhart, Nicholas of Cusa and many others. Their answer was to have recourse to the *via negativa*, but Clayton has already rejected this because its modern form seems to leave God as merely a regulative concept. He wants to both move beyond negative theology and enable us to be able to make judgements on more adequate or less adequate metaphors for God. But not only can we not have both of these options, in the end we cannot have either of them, because if all language is symbolic then it is equally so and it is not possible for us to move directly from a theory of language to making judgements in dogmatic theology. Our only recourse is to negative theology.

To conclude: the *via negativa* is inescapable for anyone who wants to think of God after Kant but remain with the great mystical strand in Christian thinking. Any move 'beyond' negative theology is ultimately impossible because, as we saw with the greatest advocates of the *via negativa*, all attempts to grasp God through language end in failure: the *via negativa* no less than the *via positiva* is negated and the end is silence. In a sceptical culture where the existence of a divine being is at best regarded as problematic and at worst a hopeless dream, negative theology frees thinking about God from too close an attachment to the images, concepts, metaphors and ideas of the Bible and the churches. The tension between the cataphatic and the apophatic, between the content of our traditions about God and the silence of our final incomprehension, is not something to be overcome but to be lived with, for it frees us from the conceit that we can, in the end, grasp the ultimate in a thought or a word.

4

Facing the Wrath of God

He is said to be justified in God's sight who is both reckoned righteous in God's judgment and has been accepted on account of his righteousness. Indeed, as iniquity is abominable to God, so no sinner can find favour in his eyes in so far as he is a sinner and so long as he is reckoned as such. Accordingly, wherever there is sin, there also the wrath and vengeance of God show themselves. (John Calvin, *Institutes of the Christian Religion*, 2000 [1559])

The Hebrew and Christian Bibles as well as the liturgy, hymnody and prayers of the Christian churches use myriad images, concepts, names and appellations for God. God is Lord, King, Shepherd, Father, Ruler, Creator, the Most High. As we would expect from a God to whom these terms are applied, God also has emotions. He (with a few exceptions God in the Bible is a 'he') gets angry and even regrets having made humans (Genesis 6.6); he sometimes seems to punish the just (Job being the greatest example); he is jealous and often seems to demand the impossible from his followers, as in the case of Abraham being asked to sacrifice Isaac (Genesis 22.1–19); he appears to delight in provoking wars or participating in them (Joshua 1.1–18; 2 Kings 19.35); he reserves the right to destroy those too obdurate to hear his message (Micah 5.9–14); he seems on occasion to refuse to listen and he retreats to sulk in silence when his people most need him (Psalm 10 chastises Yahweh for going missing in times of trouble); but he can also be kind, forgiving and even loving (Nehemiah 9.17; Isaiah 54.7–8). God seems, on the whole, to run through a wide range of emotions, many more than we would expect from a normal and reasonably balanced human being; if someone whom we knew spoke and acted like the God of the Hebrew Bible, would we ever want to be in their company?

Modern biblical scholarship can tell us that the God of the Hebrew scriptures is a composite figure, drawing on other religious traditions for some of his characteristics. The 'god of the fathers' (the God of Abraham, Isaac and Jacob), the Canaanite cosmic god 'El', the warlike Yahweh, and even the 'god of the land' Baal, influenced the development of the idea of God in the Hebrew Bible (see Eliade, 1978, pp. 162–86). The dominant picture of God combined more conceptual, cosmic elements with very human-like qualities, but the anthropomorphic qualities were very much to the fore. Yahweh, who emerges triumphant from this process of syncretism, is a God who demands absolute obedience from his followers in a somewhat despotic manner, so much so that the great scholar of religion Mircea Eliade reaches the conclusion that '[t]he intolerance and fanaticism that are characteristic of the prophets and missionaries of the three monotheisms [Judaism, Islam and Christianity] have their model and justification in Yahweh's example' (Eliade, 1978, p. 181).

In addition to these human-like characteristics, philosophers and theologians in the Christian era also attributed to God other, more abstract qualities: God is omnipotent (all-powerful); God is omniscient (all-knowing); God is uncreated; God is infinite, self-sufficient, omnipresent and eternal. God is greater than all that is or that can be, and, in the famous formulation of Saint Anselm of Canterbury in the eleventh century, God is that than which nothing greater can be thought. Nothing.

What we see in the idea of God as it has developed in the Bible and in the subsequent Christian theological tradition is that there are both anthropomorphic (attributing human qualities to God) and non-anthropomorphic terms used about God. We have images of God which originate from human ideas of personal relations, from farming, from politics, from war, from sexuality, from Babylonian creation myths and from Greek philosophy. The same God who is angry at Adam and Eve or seems to act to punish Job is also the Unmoved Mover of Aristotle and Aquinas; the God who is the lord of the heavens is also the God who sends the flood to wipe out most of his earthly creation; the God who closes the seas over the Egyptian army at the Sea of Reeds is the same God whom the Christian scripture regards as pure love (1 John 4.8). It is hardly surprising that in the early centuries of Christianity the Marcionite heresy thought that the God of the Hebrew Bible, whom they saw as characterized by anger and violence, and the God of Jesus Christ, whom they saw as characterized by compassion and love, could not possibly be the same deity.

The enigma – perhaps the tragedy – of the God of the Bible is that he must always be all of these things. The biblical God emerges alone and triumphant out of the struggle with the other gods (the gods of the Moabites and the Babylonians, of the Assyrians and the Canaanites) but in his triumph he is left alone; now he must be the source and origin of all that humankind can attribute to the deity. Here, there is no longer the possibility of recourse to the safety valve of polytheism: there is no escape such as is offered by the pantheons of Indian or Greek religion, no Shiva and Vishnu and Kali, no Apollo and Dionysius, Aphrodite and Hera. For the monotheistic religions God must encompass within one personality all the attributes which polytheism could easily diffuse throughout the pantheon; it is hardly surprising that at times it seems that all of this expectation is too much for one God. Yet, the wide variety of images used for God in the Bible and the subsequent tradition should neither surprise nor scandalize us, for how could it be otherwise? The God of monotheism must bear the weight of everything that could be thought of, attributed to, or said about the deities.

It is important to note in this regard that when talking about the God of the Hebrew Bible (the *Tanakh)* we should talk about monolatry (worship of one God from among many) as well as about monotheism (belief in the existence of only one God), recognizing that it is notoriously difficult to pinpoint a borderline between the two. The first commandment in the Decalogue warns Moses and the people: 'I am the Lord your God, who brought you out of the land of Egypt, and out of the house of bondage. You shall not have other gods before me' (Exodus 20.2–3). This is clearly a warning against choosing other gods worshipped by other nations in a polytheistic setting. God wants to be the only God in the sense of his people worshipping him alone; what gods other peoples worship is up to them. Then, in Elijah's contest with the priests of Baal (1 Kings 18.20–40), Yahweh is required to demonstrate that he is more powerful than the other gods. That is one reason why he is the one who must be worshipped; but this does not seem to exclude the existence of other deities. Deuteronomy 32 sees the 'Most High' portioning out the nations among the pantheon, and Yahweh (seen here as less than the 'Most High') is given the people of Jacob (Deuteronomy 32.8–9).

This is as clear an indication of a polytheistic context as we might find, but there are counter-indications too. For instance, while Psalm 82 sees God (*Elohim)* as supreme among the pantheon – 'God stands in the divine assembly, among the gods he dispenses justice' (Psalm 82.1) – it also asserts that the God of Israel will oversee the death of the other gods: 'You too are gods . . . but all the same, you shall die like other men' (Psalm 82.6–7). In this respect Psalm 82 seems to indicate a transition from polytheism and monolatry to monotheism. Again, in tension with polytheism is 2 Kings 5.15, where Namaan, the army commander of the king of Aram, confesses that 'there is no God in all the earth except in Israel'. And, writing around the second half of the sixth century BCE, the author of Second-Isaiah has Yahweh proclaim: 'I am Yahweh, there is no other God besides me' (Isaiah 45.5), clearly a more monotheistic statement than the Decalogue's warning against worshipping other gods. When we come to consider the case of Job, we encounter the one terrifying divine force who is attended by the other divine or semi-divine beings, including Satan, whom he rules as a despot does his court. This tension between monotheism and monolatry in the religious life of ancient Israel is not our primary concern here, except insofar as we need to be aware that Yahwism must fight to establish its place in a competitive atmosphere. And we might note the lesson of Elijah: in the Hebrew Bible these other gods may be overcome by powerful demonstrations of Yahweh's force or they may be ridiculed for their impotence, but they are not argued out of existence by the sophisticated polemics of philosophical theology.

Whether one thinks that the range of images used for God in the Bible, together with the tension between monotheistic tendencies and polytheism/monolatry, indicates a great richness in the religious life of the Jewish and Christian communities or an impossible and irresolvable confusion will depend ultimately on the perspective you take on the evidence of the texts; it can be either one or the other, or perhaps even both. Whichever stance one takes, the long history of anthropomorphism has enabled us to think that we know who God is; God has become a familiar figure, so much so that God is perceived by a major strand of Western culture in terms of a limited set of images which the tradition has used to describe God (think, for a moment of the cultural power of Michelangelo Buonarotti's striking image of God as an elderly man with a long white beard, employed in his depiction of the creation on the ceiling of the Sistine Chapel in the Vatican City, Italy). Given the cultural power of images of God as a capricious despot, a domineering father, or a benign but seldom-seen uncle (almost all such images being of a male God), many people in modern Western societies have rejected such a God, seeing in this divine character little more than an invention of a fearful human imagination, the pre-scientific worldview of a semi-nomadic and pre-scientific agrarian society onto which later, more sophisticated, cultures grafted some ideal attributes which the deity could not be without.

In the nineteenth century the German philosopher Ludwig Feuerbach defined God as simply the projection onto the absolute of human feelings and desires: God is all-knowing because we value and desire knowledge: God is all-loving because we desire to be loved; God is all-powerful because of our wish for influence and domination; God is infinite because we crave immortality, and so on. Like many moderns Feuerbach saw God as an overbearing and overweening negative influence on the human capacity for self-fulfilment: 'He who says no more of me than that I am an atheist, says and knows *nothing* of me . . . I deny God. But that means for me that I deny the negation of man' (Feuerbach, in Ayer and O'Grady, 1992, p. 131). For Feuerbach, to project our ideals onto a mythical Being is to rob human beings of their own inherent dignity; God takes from us what we owe to ourselves.

Building on Feuerbach's basic idea of projection, Sigmund Freud produced what was probably the most influential concept of God in twentieth-century Western culture, namely the idea of God as the psychological projection of the father figure, a 'big daddy' in the sky who would look after us when life was difficult and who would lay even death aside to ensure our continued existence. For Freud and his cultural interpreters, to achieve psychological wholeness we need to cast aside this angry and judgemental father figure and achieve our independence from this creation of our neurotic fear of being alone in a hostile world. In her ground-breaking work of feminist theology, *Beyond God the Father* (1986 [1973]), Mary Daly, although critical of psychoanalysis as a movement, drew upon the Freudian critique to attack images of God used to control and dominate women. Daly argued that

> if God is male, then the male is God. The divine patriarch castrates women as long as he is allowed to live on in the human imagination ... The problem is one of transforming the collective imagination so that this distortion of the human aspiration to transcendence loses its credibility. (p. 19)

As the legitimating power behind patriarchy, the domineering father figure of monotheism must be imaginatively destroyed if women are to be free.

There is much to be said in favour of these critiques by Feuerbach, Freud and others who followed in their wake. They laid bare for the first time the destructive elements in many of the concepts of God which believers encountered in the daily life of the Christian churches; they exposed the compliance of images of God with damaging psychological states; and they made possible the feminist critique of the idea of God as an all-powerful father figure, thus having a major impact on subsequent theology. Together with the other great nineteenth-century critics of religion, Marx and Nietzsche, the critiques of Feuerbach and Freud made all innocent reading of divine imagery impossible; after them we have to ask whose interest is served in using this image rather than that one; we have to ask about the political implications of thinking about God as Lord or as King or as ruler; and we have to ask honestly about the potentially damaging nature of belief in God at all, insofar as no idea or concept of God is completely innocent. It is nevertheless the case that not everyone can work out of and through damaging religious imagery to a more pure and pristine notion of the divine; and for many who have grown up in oppressive religious contexts, marked by powerful and controlling images of God, atheism has been seen as by far the more healthy psychological option.

Above all, however, what we learn from these psychological critiques is that our anthropomorphic ideas of God are always limited and inadequate; when we use human imagery to talk about God we always fail, for we use terms and ideas which are always open to misinterpretation, confusion or even abuse. But when these images become part of the permanent symbolism of the churches, and even of the wider society, they become very difficult to dislodge from their place in the consciousness of the individual or the group, and one can continue to be surprised by the often puerile and simplistic ideas of God which even otherwise well-educated people have. The main reason for this sclerosis is probably that anthropomorphism is inescapable: we cannot talk about God without using some human analogies, and it is strange if not impossible to think of the normal life of worship in Christian communities happening without the use of anthropomorphic imagery. What would be left of the language of the Christmas or Easter liturgy if all anthropomorphic imagery were removed? Very little. It would be futile, then, to rely on the Christian churches for revision of our notions of God; churches are institutions interested in survival and they are perhaps the last place we should look if we wish to re-think the very foundations of divine imagery.

Problems inevitably arise when images are understood as literal descriptions and become solidified in the popular religious consciousness. In the case of Freud, whose critique of the idea of God as a domineering father figure permeates Western culture, it is as if many who have a passing acquaintance with his theories cannot think beyond the depiction of God which he promoted. There is also a rather widespread cultural assumption that Freud succeeded in permanently separating God from mental well-being rather than seeing his theories as a critique of an inadequate concept of God by means of which Jews and Christians could reject deficient or outmoded concepts in order to discover ideas and images which more accurately reflect contemporary personal or communal experience. Yet we do not have to fall into this trap of thinking that by using certain conventional and respected words, images, ideas or perceptions of the divine we have thereby exhausted the possibilities of thinking about God. In short, in rejecting many of the outdated anthropomorphic notions of God, even by rejecting the very idea of speaking of God in anthropomorphic ways, we do not have to reject the idea of God *tout court*.

In Jewish and Christian theology there has been a long tradition of suspicion about the language which we use about God and about the ability of that language to say anything final about God or God's nature. However, this theological tradition has always existed in tension with popular and liturgical language about God which requires concrete anthropomorphic imagery to grasp the imagination and to provide a viable context for most prayer, worship and piety. Already in the Bible, despite the abundance of anthropomorphic and other imagery used about God, there is an undoubted mystery surrounding the nature of Yahweh. In his book *The Hidden Face of God* (1995), speaking of Yahweh in the context of the polytheism which marks the Bible, Richard Elliot Friedman puts it like this:

From the beginning of the book to the end, the essence of God remains unknown. Shamash is the sun. Baal is the

storm wind. Asherah is fertility. Yamm is the sea. But
what is Yahweh? Residing outside of nature, known only
through words and through acts in history, God in the
Bible remains a mystery . . . God is an enigma to humans
when in visible contact with them and is the memory of
an enigma after becoming hidden. The most that
humans are allowed to know is the outward personality
of Yahweh: a merciful and gracious God, long-suffering,
abundant in kindness . . . But what Yahweh *is* is the
Bible's unspoken, pervasive mystery. (Friedman, 1995,
p. 117).

Friedman has somewhat neglected Yahweh's less attractive,
aggressive qualities but either way, as the prophet Isaiah
says, God is indeed a hidden God (Isaiah 45.15).

In separate works, Friedman and Jack Miles (Miles, 1995)
have claimed that, as the Hebrew Bible progresses, God
actually disappears from the text and in the later books of the
Bible he ceases to act in the ways that he had acted in the
earlier books. To understand how this could be the case, it is
important to note that the *Tanakh,* as it has been assembled
by its final redactor, ends with the books of Esther, Daniel,
Ezra-Nehemiah and 1 & 2 Chronicles – accounts of everyday
human affairs – and not with the so-called 'minor prophets'
which end the Christian Old Testament. The last direct
words of God in the *Tanakh* come well before the end and
they constitute the bombastic rantings out of the whirlwind
designed to force the just man Job into quivering submission
before the Almighty.

Job was the servant of the Lord, about whom God boasts to
Satan: 'Have you noticed my servant Job, and that there is no
one on earth like him, blameless and upright, fearing God
and avoiding evil?' (Job 1.8). But the Lord is jibed by Satan
into handing Job over to the power of the evil one, and a bet
ensues over Job's loyalty: will he or will he not curse the

Lord? And so, while trusting in the God who could not resist Satan's enticement into testing his goodness, Job loses almost everything. Yet despite all his misfortunes, the loss of his children, his prosperity and his reputation, Job does not curse God – as Satan wagered – but he continues to berate him, to harangue him and to question his justice.

The Lord is enraged by Job's impudence, and much like a powerful human person who is embarrassed by their inadequacies or duplicities being exposed, the Lord reacts in a fit of self-righteous anger. Job, by now at the end of his physical and mental strength, is subjected to an overwhelming demonstration of the power of God. With his last speech in the *Tanakh* God presents himself, as Miles puts it, 'with withering sarcasm and towering bravado, as an amoral, irresistible force' (Miles, 1995, p. 315). The Lord interrogates Job: 'Where were you when I laid the foundation of the earth? Tell me, if you have understanding. Who determined its measurements – surely you know! Or who stretched the [measuring] line upon it? . . . Have you commanded the morning since your days began, and caused the dawn to know its place?' (Job 38.4–5, 12). God boasts of his power over the weather and over the stars, of his knowledge of agriculture, his prowess at providing food for the lions and the ravens, and of his knowledge of the breeding habits of mountain goats. The Lord's speech about his greatness compared to the feebleness of Job's humanity are words of immense power and beauty, but they can only mask and not supplant the gloating braggadocio of God. Job is impressed, but he is not overwhelmed.

Faced with this barrage of evidence, Job is commanded to respond: 'Shall a faultfinder contend with the Almighty? Anyone who argues with God must respond' (Job 40.2). Job's response is one of almost silent bewilderment, the words of an almost broken man: 'See, I am of small account; what shall I answer you? I lay my hand on my mouth. I have spoken

once, and I will not answer; twice, but will proceed no further'
(Job 40.4–5). The silence of Job prefigures the forthcoming
silence of God, yet Job's very weakness is his strength. In his
justness and righteousness, Job is feeble before the might of
God yet exposes power for what it is: empty without justice.
Job thus unmasks the God of the Hebrew Bible in his
dealings with humanity. When faced with a God who is a God
of power without also being a God of justice, human beings
have the right to demand an answer. If, as Miles suggests,
Satan is not another being but the darker side of the divine
personality, then in the end when God relents and restores
Job's fortune (although he does not get his children back) it is
a victory for humanity. In the face of the innocence of Job, God
has discovered something about himself, and in the end it is
not the righteousness of Job which is at issue but the righteousness of God (Miles, 1995, p. 326).

Perhaps the most important lesson of the Book of Job is the
change which it brings about in the very character of God. As
Miles puts it, after his dealings with Job, 'the Lord can never
seem quite the same to himself. The devil is now a permanent
part of his reality; and though at the eleventh hour he has
broken free from the Adversary, he has done so through a
deeper humiliation at the hands of a terrestrial adversary,
Job himself' (p. 327). As the *Tanakh* hones its concept of God,
as the Lord gradually takes over the powers and roles of the
competing deities, eventually in Job the final, anguished, possibility is confronted: is the Lord the source and origin of evil
as well as of good? Of course in relenting to spare Job and his
friends the text tells us that the good side of God wins out, but
we are left with a bitter aftermath. Job receives financial
compensation as well as the company of his brothers and
sisters, but how is this to compensate him for the loss of his
original family? The author of the Book of Job leaves us
holding on to one final thought: why is it that Job suffered
because of his goodness, for after all it was his very probity

which led the Lord to boast of him to Satan? Can it ever be that for the believer, goodness is its own reward?

God's last word in the *Tanakh* is not to his servant Job but to Eliphaz the Temanite, the friend of Job, who is chastised for speaking badly of the Lord. Irritable to the end, as a parting shot the Lord orders Eliphaz to make a burnt offering for himself and the other 'friends' of Job. Amazingly and brazenly, after all that has passed between them, God asks Job to pray for his 'friends' in order for them to gain his (God's) forgiveness. And then he is gone. In later books such as the Book of Chronicles, God's earlier speeches are recalled; in Daniel he seems to do miraculous things but is truly a distant God serene on his throne; in Esther and the Song of Songs he is not spoken of at all; he is referred to in Ecclesiastes, Lamentations and Nehemiah, but he himself remains mute. Who, in the end, has reduced whom to silence? (Miles, 1995, p. 329).

In the literary analysis of the *Tanakh* offered by Friedman and Miles, the God who acts so powerfully in the creation of the world, in the election of Abraham, in the Exodus of his people from Egypt, in the giving of the law, and in the conquest of the land, eventually fades from the scene until in the later books he is no longer the central character, and the lives of people move along under their own capacities and effort rather than through the sway and intervention of Yahweh. Friedman brings together the theological, literary and historical reasons for God's gradual occlusion in the *Tanakh*:

Monotheism plus history plus factors of psychology meant perceiving the age of power, the great age of closeness with the deity, as behind us and always receding . . . No matter at what point a biblical author (and that author's audience) lived, if the author was writing about historical ages long past he or she would conceive of God

as present and involved in human affairs. When writing
of more and more contemporary history, the author
would see God as less involved, as the evidence of contemporary events (setbacks, apparent rarity of miracles)
attested. And when writing of the distant future, the
author could again conceive of the deity as visibly
involved . . . Through this quite amazing combination of
factors, the story of the relations between God and
humans in the Hebrew Bible came to include the disappearance of God. (Friedman, 1995, p. 95)

The Lord's dealings with Job are, from this perspective,
central to understanding the God of the Bible. In the final
redaction of the Hebrew Bible, humans gain control over the
course of events as God recedes from the action. Unlike the
organization of the canonical books of the Christian Old Testament, God does not end the drama with the words of his
prophets. Rather he is constrained to accede to the humdrum
round of temporal and everyday events: in the sexual exuber-
ance of the Song of Songs, in the orderly family life of the
Book of Ruth, and in the practical affairs of administration in
the Book of Nehemiah, humans reassert their autonomy, and
there is not another Job who has to justify himself before
God; that battle has been fought and Job won. Paradoxically,
though, it is this very ordinariness of events after the trau-
matic climax of God's encounter with the good man Job that
permits God to carry on. In Miles' words, 'the otherwise
deathly silence of the Lord God [is] covered over by the rising
bustle and hum of real life'; it is this return to the mundane
which in the end saves God's life (see Miles, 1995, p. 405). By
refusing to allow a tragic ending with the defeat of God by
Job, the *Tanakh* enables God to be saved by a less than
graceful withdrawal from the stage. The Hebrew Bible ends,
as Friedman puts it, 'with a mysterious God who has hidden
the divine face from humans, leaving them in apparent

charge of their world' (1995, p. 117). Part of the legacy of the *Tanakh* to subsequent Judaism and to Christianity was this mysterious, concealed and occluded God.

On the basis of this, we might surmise that the idea of the God of monotheism is unsustainable when thought of in anthropomorphic terms. If we learn from Job that God contains the origin of good and of evil, is it not inevitable that this God would have to withdraw from direct contact with humanity, for his affairs with humans could only result in disaster? Maybe this withdrawal became inevitable when God was perceived as capable of acting in history, for with the rejection of polytheism in Israel, God was forced to do the impossible and take unto himself all the powers and forces of the deities. This was at first an important step forward, for a God who was not tied to the sun or to the seasons, who was not confined to expressing himself solely through the power of the wind or through the ocean or through the fires of lightning, was free to act in history through contact with his chosen people, and for this reason it is God's *word* that is all important. But eventually the freedom and power of God to speak to his people, to make deals with them, to chastise, cajole, encourage, reprimand, punish and endear himself to them, came to be God's misfortune, for a God who had all the powers at his disposal, yet was thought of in anthropomorphic terms, would find it difficult in the long term to rein in his actions. Like any powerful human being, God must have his way, but it is with Job that he finally goes too far and makes a pact with the devil or, if we wish, gives in to the darker side of his own character and seeks to test the one man who could stand up to him. His boast about Job's goodness becomes his own undoing.

In the end, for anyone interested in understanding how we might think of God today, the most intriguing aspect of this analysis of God's occlusion within the *Tanakh* lies not in its historical or literary import but in the theological insights which we can gain from it. Long before Nietzsche proclaimed God's death, God's own people saw him as fading from the scene. Job's triumph over the majesty of God is that Job in the end is convinced of his own righteousness, for there is no other recourse. The lesson of the final redaction of the *Tanakh* is that humans do not have to be overwhelmed by the might and majesty of God, yet we can continue to live in the shadow of the silent God without ever thinking that God is gone for good. Perhaps, as Miles suggests, God loses interest in the story, but this could only be part of the explanation. Is it not also the case that God's people had to distance themselves from God, for who could live for long with the all-action character of Genesis and Exodus? In the eighteenth century David Hume pointed out that miracles always seemed to have happened to other people in other places a long time ago, and it would seem that God's own people occasionally thought along the same lines. It is commonplace for us to read the *Tanakh* and to see it permeated with the divine presence, but the truth is that for much of the time the question is: where has God gone, and how can we live without him? Ours is not the first culture to experience the divine absence.

As I pointed out at the beginning of this chapter, the Bible contains both anthropomorphic and non-anthropomorphic images of God. If it is impossible to speak about and to God without using human images, values, ideas and concepts to depict the divine character, it is also dangerous to do so. The real pitfall always comes into view when the anthropomorphic God is perceived as acting with the powers attributed to the cosmic God. As I have tried to demonstrate, the epitome of this happening in the Bible is the case of Job, who discovers to his cost that God likes a wager and the result is a frightening expression of God's might, anger and cruelty. For us, this dilemma remains inescapable: how do we think of God as personal without attributing to God all the qualities of a despot?

The answer, I think, lies in what we understand when we speak of our relation to the divine as personal, and whether we consider this to be primarily a statement about God or a statement about ourselves. If it is a statement about God then how can we ever escape the pitfalls of anthropomorphism with all that that entails? How could we avoid, like Job, encountering the force and might of a God who might only be the projection of our own inadequacies and who in the end can only be a terrifying idol? If, however, all talk of God as personal is recognized as talk only about ourselves, about our personal relation to what is deepest in humanity, and about our longing for ultimate meaning, then we have little to fear from such a God. Like Job, we can come to understand our own innocence with regard to God by not giving in to the powerful image of an angry and despotic deity. Unlike him, though, we now have the freedom to imagine the divine as always beyond all our ideas, concepts and projections. Who knows? We might just find this possibility liberating, including those of us who rightly reject the idol so often presented to us in the synagogues and churches.

In the end, Job teaches us to keep our dignity in the face of power and violence, even when that power and violence is attributed to the most powerful Being imaginable. In that respect he could be a model for us all, more worthy of our respect and esteem than the God at whose hands he suffers. The lesson of the Book of Job is not primarily about the suffering of the innocent, but about the nature of the anthropomorphic God. As the author of Job never lets us forget, bad things do happen to good people, and, for those who believe in a God of providence who acts in history, this is God's Achilles heel. In the end, after the treatment meted out to Job, when God withdrew from the scene, we might perhaps hope that he did so in penitence and shame.

5

Divine Consolation?

If you ask your earthly father for a loaf do you get a stone? If you ask your earthly father for a fish do you get a snake? If you ask your heavenly Father for anything at all will you not get it? (John Dominic Crossan, *The Essential Jesus*, 1994, p. 115 [Cf. Matthew 7.9–11])

In his book *Why Christianity Must Change or Die* (1998), Episcopalian bishop John Shelby Spong relates the event in his life which for him placed 'one final nail' in the coffin of the God of classical theism. In 1981 his wife Joan developed cancer which was diagnosed as probably fatal. As the Spongs were a very well-known Christian family in New Jersey, large numbers of public and private prayers were said on her behalf in hundreds of churches in the diocese of Newark and beyond. Bishop Spong's wife lived for six and a half years before finally succumbing to the disease.

During that period, as the length of her remission increased, many of those who had prayed for her recovery began to believe that their prayers were being answered and that God was healing her from the cancer. But in quiet moments Bishop Spong had his doubts. What, he wondered, would happen to the wife of a sanitation worker in the city of Newark who was given the same diagnosis and whose family was not well known in the Christian community or who were perhaps not religious at all? Would she have less time to live because no one was praying for her? Would she experience more pain because the attention of the deity was not oriented towards her but towards someone who had prayers said on their behalf? Could the bishop place his trust in a God who behaved so capriciously, favouring some humans over others on the basis of their social, religious or economic status in the community? The answer to all of these questions was, in his own words, 'No, no, a thousand times no! If that was where praying to a theistic God wound up, then dismissing such a distorted concept from organized religion was not a loss, but a positive gain' (p. 142).

In Spong's view the God of traditional Christianity, who intervenes in our world on behalf of those who pray to him, becomes a monstrosity when we think of the immensity of human suffering. It is not so much the question as to why God permits suffering, but rather that the belief of Christianity that God can and has intervened in the affairs of human beings ends up as simply beyond our comprehension when we ask on what grounds God has decided to intervene in case A rather than in case B, or why God has decided to help person X rather than person Y? If the answer is that it was simply the power of prayer, then we are left with new questions. How many prayers, said by whom, and at what time, should we expect to be effective and in what cases? Why is it that those people lucky enough to be born into a Christian culture have access to the power of the true God and everyone else has to make do with an inadequate notion of God or maybe no God at all? Why would God answer the prayers of one person and then not answer the prayers of their neighbour who prayed with her or him for a different intention? Why can God not answer all prayers (which would most surely result in a very religious human population indeed)?

When we ask these questions in this way we can see that this concept of praying to the God of intervention belongs to a magical concept of the world: somehow our prayers and supplications reach their target, they are couched in such a way as to have an effect on the will of God, to persuade the deity to change the malignant cells to healthy ones. This God seems to belong in the realm of animist beliefs: forces in the world are viewed as having personal powers; because persons are the entities most familiar to us, we attribute person-like actions to other entities, including God. Not only is this notion of God and of prayer demeaning to human beings, who become supplicants at the feet of an infinitely powerful force, with the option of life and death over us, but it is also damaging to the idea of God. One person with whom I recently discussed the effectiveness of prayer put it to me in words similar to these: 'Who, in a modern, educated population which knows the scientific basis of the pathology of disease and understands the functioning of the planet's weather systems, could believe in a Super Being who decides to cure this person's illness and not that one, or who decides to end the drought here and not there just because someone somewhere decided to pray for intervention? If this is God then Freud was right, and God is nothing more than a projection of the idea of the father figure who will make everything all right, a king whom we approach like supplicants and who hands out favours here and there on little more than a whim.'

For many modern people, like Bishop Spong and my interlocutor, to believe in the benevolent, providential, interventionist God of theism is to be forced to accept too much on trust, to go against what the evidence of one's senses and one's experience says about a world in which miraculous divine intervention does not occur. To accept this God is to approve of theological rationalizations which themselves have no warrant other than the fact that they can function to preserve the faith of the believer when otherwise all would be lost. From this perspective, the God of classical theism is not disproved but simply becomes too improbable to be believed in in the way in which both popular Christianity and much of the formal theological tradition have understood God. Spong's theological views are nothing new; they have been around among theologians since the 'death of God' movement in the 1960s. What is interesting, however, is that these views are coming more to the fore among believing Christians, including bishops. Is this a sign that parts of the Christian community are beginning, slowly, to abandon belief in God as a transcendent Being?

Yet this God of intervention in the physical world is the God whom most Christians have believed in and, at least for those who make prayers of petition, continue to believe in. Yet when we think of what we expect of God conceived in this way, we see that Spong is correct: God thus understood becomes an ethical affront to our sense of justice and fairness. If this God were a human being, would we not most likely condemn him for his callousness and inconstancy in the face of the immense suffering which we can still witness daily? Perhaps the power of such an image of God has faded somewhat from our collective consciousness, as we rely more and more on our own powers of manipulation of the natural world to predict natural disasters and to cure illness, but it is not so long ago in Western culture that the power and will of God were looked to as an explanation for everything that we ourselves could not comprehend.

This was brought home forcefully to me by a small incident which I saw on British television two or three years ago. A well-known British journalist and writer, who had covered the Soviet Union's war in Afghanistan, adopted two young orphan boys and brought them back with him to the West to start a new life. The boys had been raised to that point as Muslims but it seemed, from the evidence of the documentary, that they were no longer being raised religiously. One evening their new guardian suggested that they spend the next day out of the house because the weather forecast suggested a fine day. This proposal brought howls of incredulity,

even derision, from the boys. Their reaction was occasioned
by the idea that someone could tell in advance what the
weather was going to be like: how could any human being
forecast the weather, for the sun and the wind are completely
dependent upon the will of Allah. Seeing this small domestic
event with theological overtones was like looking into the
past of our own history, when it was possible for a majority of
people to believe that the will of God had a direct impact on
the most mundane things in everyday life.

Yet this criticism of an interventionist view of God is dis-
turbing to many people, for without belief in a God who can
effect changes in the course of events in this world, what is
left of prayer and evocation; what is left of the cries of the
afflicted to heaven? All that can be left is that the power of
prayer for those who are ill, for the success of the harvest, or
for success in battle, comes not from the influence which it
has on a deity who will occasionally deign to intervene and
adjust the course of nature, but comes rather from the human
realization that we are not alone in our pain, that we are
cared for by those to whom we are close, that our continued
well-being and very existence is of untold value to all those
who love us. That is all. But is it not, ultimately, a far, far
more profound experience to know that we are loved by other
human beings than to think that we may or may not merit
the healing touch or warlike action of a whimsical deity? If we
can believe that God also loves us, then that is an additional
bonus, but I know few people who could count themselves
among those who *truly* believe that God could or will act
directly to save the harvest in Bangladesh, make the rains
fall on Somalia, or keep American military personnel safe in
action. In the Gulf War, were not the Iraqi soldiers also
praying to God?

Without the interventionist God of classical theism and
popular piety, the philosophical–theological 'problem of evil'
is revealed as a non-problem. As it is normally expressed, the

problem of evil exposes the tension, or paradox, between the power and the goodness of the God of theism. As there is evil in the world (so-called ontic or non-moral evil, such as natural disasters, and moral evil perpetrated by human beings) we can ask why God does nothing about it: is God unable to act to prevent it, in which case God is not all-powerful; or is God unwilling to, in which case God is not all-good? The conclusion reached by the advocates of this argument is that either way the credibility and existence of the theistic God is undermined, if not disproved altogether.

A standard theological response to this problem is that God has given us free will and that therefore moral evil is to be expected; in Christian theology the fall of humanity through disobedience to God is considered to be the origin of moral evil. This argument is often complemented by the 'vale of tears' or 'soul-building' argument, which tries to persuade us that God permits moral evil in order to allow us the scope to grow spiritually, and by the theological argument that God suffered with us by taking human form in the person of Jesus Christ. In this view suffering is itself redemptive and as a religious perspective on our condition it is both moving and consoling to the (Christian) believer.

A more sophisticated way of understanding the question of suffering from a theistic perspective comes from theologians who have reflected on the meaning of God in a universe which has taken such a long time to produce self-conscious beings through the process of evolution. The argument runs that we should not think of God's freedom to create as freedom in a complete and absolute sense, as if God were capable of creating any universe at all. Rather, it might be the case that, in order to allow for the possibility of self-conscious and morally aware beings to emerge, God had to create a universe with certain characteristics; if a highest value for God is the existence of free beings who can come to know and under-stand God, then for us to be here, the world has to be like this, and that includes the suffering that we and other creatures endure. Perhaps we could imagine a better universe, one in which suffering was much diminished or even absent, but it is not one in which we could exist. Therefore, we would have to acknowledge that from the perspective of our own emergence through evolution, this is the best possible world (see Ward, 1998, pp. 93–6).

Like the other theodicy arguments, this viewpoint does help to make sense of suffering from the perspective of someone who believes in the creator God for whatever reason; as it is a fact that we took a very long time indeed to emerge through the evolutionary process, any theological explanation of suffering has to take that into account, and it therefore makes sense to think of the world which we inhabit as the best world in which beings like us could evolve. Such an explanation, however, does not necessarily work to make it more attractive to believe in God despite the suffering in the world, but it may allow the believer to see that God could not have created a world just like this one without the pain and suffering; such a painless world would not be the world we know and would not have human beings as we know them. It is, indeed, difficult to imagine what a world that operated according to natural laws of physics and included free moral beings yet did not include suffering would be like. In this limited respect, Leibniz was correct: for us, serendipitous products of evolution, this is the best of all possible worlds. It is so, however, not because of the logical need for God to make just this world and no other, but simply because it is the world that has produced us.

While it is obvious to us all that we can sometimes learn from pain and from suffering, one does not need to be a theist to understand this. In addition, while we must also take seriously the use and misuse of our free will, as an answer to the question of evil these philosophical and theological arguments are unlikely to be persuasive for anyone who cannot already claim to have experienced the love and compassion of a personal God. Viewed from outside the parameters of religious belief, such arguments can only appear as rationalizations which seek to defend the theistic God at all costs. Further, the 'problem of evil' is only a problem in relation to a God who may or may not interfere in the natural world; when, as in the case of Bishop Spong, this form of belief is abandoned, then the need to reconcile evil with an all-good and powerful interventionist God disappears, and there is no longer any need for a theodicy which attempts to justify God in the face of suffering and evil. Then we can see suffering for what it is – an inescapable part of our world and our human condition – and we can be free to struggle against it without thinking that we have to reconcile it with our belief in a God of interference and intervention who loves us but still chooses to leave us in our misery.

Furthermore, even if we were to take the strictly theological arguments seriously, they seem to me to act as much against the benevolence of God as in favour of it. After all, if God has suffered with us in the person of Jesus Christ and his death on the cross, why should we in any way find this comforting? What impact can a short period of even intense suffering have on the all-powerful creator of the universe (in this regard we can understand the attraction of the view of the Gnostics and other heterodox groups in early Christianity that Christ had only *appeared* to suffer on the cross, for the divine nature could never be reduced to the blood and filth involved in the crucifixion of a common criminal)? Are we to be persuaded by the view that God suffered in the person of Jesus and still suffers with us in our pain, and that this somehow makes our own suffering okay? Are we to think that the death of Jesus on the cross is enough to offer comfort to the parents of a child suffering from leukaemia or to someone dying in unmitigated agony from AIDS or the Ebola virus?

I would emphasize that I am not saying here that the 'problem of evil' argument – which claims that God cannot be both all-good and all-powerful – succeeds in disproving the existence of God, as many of its proponents think. Logical arguments against God's existence which attempt to exploit the tension between God's power and God's goodness fail to convince, because it is always possible to add another nuance to what exactly one intends when one says the word 'God'; a subtle shift in the description of the divine nature or concept of divine action moves the target, so to speak. So, faced with the challenge that God cannot be both all-good and all-powerful – as classic theism claims – believers can readily have recourse to the explanation that God's will is simply inscrutable; what God chooses to do or not to do is his decision alone and is not to be questioned by us. For those who already believe in God, this is a perfectly acceptable explanation or justification of God's apparent inactivity in the face of enormous suffering and evil.

In his book *Letter to a Man in the Fire: Does God Exist and Does He Care?* – an insightful and poignant reflection on the nature and meaning of suffering from a broadly Christian perspective – the American poet and writer Reynolds Price addresses the issue of God's existence and providence in an open letter to a 35-year-old cancer sufferer who had written to him having heard about Price's own struggle with the disease. Price believes firmly in the existence and ultimate benevolence of God, yet rejects the theological argument that God suffers alongside us and that we should be comforted by this; he regards these arguments as 'more nearly exercises in a near-medieval narrative fantasy than the results of patient commonsensical observation of the world and its creatures' (Price, 1999, p. 58). Price's own view – this is the view of a man who suffered painfully from cancer of the spine and lost the use of his legs – is that there is a living Creator whom he has experienced powerfully in his life (most notably in a vision of Jesus who washed the cancer wound in his spine), but that this God sometimes chooses not to be involved with his creatures: 'In times of his absence or silence, I've never felt that he was prevented from reaching me, only that he was choosing his distance and for unstated reasons' (Price, 1999, p. 58).

But why would God want to withdraw his attention from someone to whom he had at other times been very close, or why would he wish to give care and attention to some creatures and not to others? Price puzzles over this: 'It has seemed to me for years that there may well be many human beings of whom the Creator takes sporadic notice' (p. 36). He rejects the Calvinist doctrine of predestination as too destructive of human freedom, and speculates, along with Milton in *Paradise Lost,* on an idea found in the thirteenth-century esoteric Kabbalist text, the *Zohar,* in which God announces that in order for there to be something which is not God, he must withdraw from creation and not fill it completely with the divine presence. While these are interesting theological speculations, they seem to me to be of little help to us in attempting to understand what God could have to do with our suffering here and now: the mystery of reconciling suffering with the care of a personal God remains unresolved, for to think of God as caring yet choosing on occasion not to care seems to leave us with the very worst aspects of an anthropomorphic God. In the end, Price's conviction of God's benevolence and care comes down to his 'bafflement' at how anyone could be an atheist and to his own intense experience of how the pain and suffering of life can be given meaning through belief.

Yet, while Price is a believer, he is no romantic idealist: he holds out hope for the resurrection, that 'singular occasion of extraordinary promise for our earthly lives and thereafter', but he acknowledges that this personal conviction is 'no feather bed . . . [and] no opiate' (p. 73). He faces up to the pos-

sibility that all good and all evil come from God and that the
divine will is in the end inscrutable (shades here, perhaps, of
his Calvinist background). He faces the dark prospect that
God is 'all enduring things – both what we humans perceive
as good and evil: birth, growth, flowering, decline, agony, dev-
astation, death' (p. 75). He wonders what it would be like if
we had been allowed in our worship to think of God as
somewhat like Brahman is in Hinduism; what if God were
the origin of 'all things, creative and destructive, to his creatures and that each of these things is *good,* whatever our
immediate evaluation of it, and good precisely because it is
the will of that Father and in some way fulfills the intent of
his ongoing care for all that exists?' (pp. 76–7).

Price goes further: what if we were to think of all that we
consider *evil* (with the exception, he avers, of that which comes
from other people, living creatures or simple accidents – but
why not include those as well?) as coming from the will of God.
What if we were to consider illness and disease as God's will
'and thus not subject to protest or complaint from us but only to
whatever solace or exultance we may take in perceiving that
our lives are in God's hands and are the object of his conscious
will, however terrible in the short run?' (p. 77). This is a coura-
geous and forceful creed: give in to the will of God, accept all
things, and accept them as somehow good in the long term. It is,
perhaps, the sort of insight given only to those who have
suffered a great deal, those who can envision the possibilities in
suffering in a way that others cannot. Price manages to avoid
the classical formulation of the problem of evil insofar as he
brings evil into the will of God and thereby avoids blaming a
wholly good God for a world of pain and anguish. He asks,
somewhat plaintively: 'What dictionary, in all the world, can
give us a definition of *father* that even begins to hint at the
deepest dark in the nature of what is called – most perilously –
God the Father? (p. 78). God is saved from our anger at a world
of suffering, but at a cost, for in the end he does not try to justify

God but has God encompass all of reality, good and evil.

Price candidly realizes the absurdity involved in this form of belief, quoting with approval Tertullian's defiant *credo quia absurdum est* ('I believe because it is absurd'). This is belief at perhaps its most stark and its most honest, but is it more convincing as a response than that of Bishop Spong to the possible effect of prayer on his wife's illness? Which option we find the more convincing will not be decided by rational argument but by our own emotional and affective reaction to the events of our lives. Like Price, I find the theological arguments for a God who suffers with us to be unconvincing, perhaps even bordering on the insulting, and yet how difficult it is to believe in a God who is the source of both good and evil. Surely our response to this God could just as readily be hatred as love, for there is no lack of evil for us to attribute to the deity. Price only defends this God by appealing to his darker nature and to his inscrutable will, but is this a God in whom we could place our unbounded confidence and trust?

A very different, but equally moving view of the meaning of suffering is offered by British writer and journalist John Diamond. Writing in the London *Observer* newspaper on 31 December 2000, Diamond discussed the question of the meaning of life posed to him by his editor: 'What is the point of it all?' Diamond responded by telling his own story:

My position is this: I have an apparently terminal disease which doesn't allow me to make any realistic plans for more than a couple of months ahead, a voice which stopped when my cancerous tongue was removed, a diet entirely dependent on the food blender, and a fair to middling amount of pain on most days. To add insult to cancerous injury, I neither feel the need of nor can I discover any comfort in religious faith . . . and yet most of the time, and within the usual limits, I seem to be happy.

Diamond reflects on the meaning of his life in the light of his own suffering, the possibility that it will end very soon, the family he would leave behind, and comes to his own conclusion about the meaning of it all:

This is what it's all about . . . It's about getting angry with me for having different opinions from yours or not expressing the ones you have as well as you would have expressed them. It's about the breakfast you've just had and the dinner you're going to have. It's about the random acts of kindness which still, magically, preponderate over acts of incivility or nastiness. It's about rereading *Great Expectations* and . . . about being able to watch old episodes of Frasier on satellite TV whenever we want, having the choice of three dozen breakfast cereals . . . It's about loving and being loved, about doing the right thing, about one day being missed when we're gone. And that's all it's about. It isn't about heaven and hell or the love of Christ or Allah or Yahweh because even if those things do exist, they don't have to exist for us to get on with it. (Diamond, *The Observer*, 31 December 2000)

This one person's lack of need for any religious comfort in his suffering is not offered as a philosophical argument; it is simply a very personal perspective, a response to his own particular life and painful circumstances. Yet, in his calmness and courage, Diamond demonstrates how it is possible to have equanimity and peace in the face of suffering and death without recourse to God or any form of religious consolation. If Bishop Spong rejects a God who seems to arbitrarily choose whom to heal, and if Reynolds Price finds his suffering explained through his own interpretation of a God who chooses to notice some and not others, Diamond feels no need for religious comfort of any sort; he is content with the joy of the everyday events of life, choosing to find solace in the mundane.

John Diamond's encounter with serious illness and his reflection on the meaning of life in the light of his own mortality, as he recounts it, reveals the importance, even necessity, of *personal* religious experience if someone is to make sense of suffering from a religious perspective. Even in the face of death, this one person who is well informed intellectually about religion does not find any personal comfort in these beliefs. Even if God existed, Diamond reflects, he himself would have to get on with living everyday life, and the implication is that God could have little effect on how he would deal with that.

Diamond's phlegmatic response to his illness is a reminder of the wonder which the death of the philosopher David Hume evoked for many of his contemporaries in the eighteenth century. Hume was well known as an unbeliever, and when word got out that he was dying, it naturally raised for many the question as to whether he would turn to religion in his final days. The economist Adam Smith, a friend of Hume's who visited him during his final illness, reported in a letter to William Strahan of Hume's attitude in the face of his approaching demise:

> [T]hough he found himself much weaker, yet his cheerfulness never abated, and he continued to divert himself, as usual, with correcting his own works for a new edition, with reading books of amusement, with the conversation of his friends; and, sometimes in the evening, with a party at his favourite game of whist. His cheerfulness was so great, and his conversation and amusements run so much in their usual strain, that, notwithstanding all bad symptoms, many people could not believe he was dying.

Smith reports Hume as saying 'I am dying as fast as my enemies, if I have any, could wish, and as easily and cheerfully as my best friends could desire' (Smith, in Knight and Herrick, 1995, p. 69). Hume, like Diamond after him and like many, many others, did not need or expect to be comforted in their pain by God or any other form of religious belief.

It is clear that resolution and courage in the face of illness and imminent death are not the sole preserve of the religious believer. Any talk of God's love for and comfort of the sick and dying only makes sense on an individual level, not in any general terms which could be applied to everyone who suffers (namely, all of us). To put this in the theological terms of Christianity, in the absence of someone's real and personal experience of the comfort of God, or the love of Christ, or the consolation of the Holy Spirit, all talk of God's love for humanity means very little. Theologians may speak lyrically of God's love for the whole creation or for the human family in particular; but this love, if it exists at all, can only be experienced by individual human beings in the very particular circumstances of their individual lives. Some, like Reynolds Price, have that experience even to an intense degree which gives coherence to the whole of experience and life; others, like Bishop Spong, find that illness, suffering and death are the very point at which the meaning of the very concept of God breaks down; and some others, like John Diamond, see no need or desire for such love, relying instead on the simple comforts of ordinary temporal existence.

Which of these is the 'better' or more 'true' response to pain and to suffering? There is no answer to that question other than to say that each person's response is legitimate in its own right. Perhaps there is a God who chooses to give comfort to some and not to others as Price thinks; or, perhaps there is no such transcendent God and we should learn to gain comfort from the idea that God is simply a part of what we ourselves are, as Spong asserts; or, with John Diamond, we should perhaps look on all such beliefs with a sceptical eye and gain as much pleasure and purpose as we can from the simple events which fill the remaining days that we have on this planet. There is no magical key which would enable us to judge which option is the better one.

To re-emphasize a point already made: if God is to be thought of as real, existing, transcendent Being, then God can only be believed in by the individual human person, not rationalized or generalized as a principle which could be applied to everybody. It is an understandable temptation of the religious believer to speak of the love or comfort of God as if that were something available to everyone. But this is patently not the case, and from within the Christian perspective Reynolds Price comes closest to an honest appraisal of the matter when he speculates that God may offer his love to some and not to others. Yet, even for the believer, this view of God caring for some and not for others must be difficult to maintain. From the perspective of the sceptic or the unbeliever, of course, such talk makes little sense; it can only be surmised that either God does not exist or that God exists in such a mode as to make the possibility of God's care for individual human beings unlikely. For the sceptic or unbeliever, a view expressed so well by John Diamond, evil and suffering are simply part of the reality of things and we have to get on with living with that. God is peripheral to our own struggle.

Raymond Carver's powerful though desolate short story, 'A Small Good Thing' (1994 [1988]), portrays how consolation in suffering may come from the most unexpected and most mundane of sources. Howard and Ann Weiss have their comfortable middle-class life come tumbling down around them when their son Scotty is hit by a passing car on his birthday. The boy later loses consciousness and, after a few days in hospital during which the doctors assure the parents that he will soon wake up, he dies. In their desperation the parents mouth some perfunctory prayers and Ann even envies another mother who is praying fervently for her son who was wounded in a stabbing. But Ann's prayers seem to float into empty space; they appear more as a cultural knee-jerk reaction in a crisis, rather than a real act of faith.

Then, during the period Scotty is in hospital struggling for his life, the parents receive a series of curt telephone calls which in their pain and disorientation they interpret as cruel harassment. The calls are from the baker from whom they ordered the boy's birthday cake; but the baker, an inarticulate man who is ill at ease in normal conversation, fails abjectly to communicate the reason for the calls, and appears to the parents to be the perpetrator of a cruel joke as he chastises them for forgetting their son's birthday.

When, after Scotty's death, the parents realize finally who made the calls, their anger and frustration focus on the baker and they confront him in his bakery in the middle of the night. Yet, at the point of greatest potential conflict, a 'small good thing' happens: the baker apologizes for his part in their anguish and offers them coffee and cinnamon rolls while he tells them about his life and how he came to be the person he is. The moment of anger passes and the story ends with all three talking until dawn, not thinking of leaving. In this bleak narrative of modern life without religion, there is no happy ending. Both Scotty and Franklin, the stabbed boy, die; prayer has no effect. There is no consolation other than a small moment of human contact over coffee and rolls.

Carver's postmodern, post-Christian narrative is a sad story of anguish and mutual miscomprehension, yet it offers a vision of the only solace the author thinks possible in a godless world. Only in the smallest act of human kindness, as in the offer of a cinnamon roll, is consolation possible. In a world without God, the story suggests, the best we can hope for in our pain and suffering is some fleeting moment of human contact, when barriers are broken down, and we console each other in the smallest of ways.

It is surely the case that no amount of persuasion and argument – no matter how philosophically clever – can convince people to believe in something that they do not experience. Whether one's response to suffering is more akin to that of Spong, Price, Diamond or Carver will depend on factors far deeper and more profound than philosophical or theological conundrums about the power and goodness of God set over and against the evils of the world. It depends on our reaction to our whole existence – emotional, physical, social and cognitive – and on our capacity to find some meaning in even the darkest moments. It will depend on how each of us creates meanings which sustain us through joy and sadness and it will depend on what we hope for and expect from our lives and from the universe as we experience it.

This view may seem very unsatisfactory to those who think that we either need or can have some form of cognitive certainty about God. Yet it is the only view that we can hold with consistency. Religious believers may think that there is no solace for suffering and death other than the compassion of a transcendent God, but it is clear that recourse to God offers solace to some and not to others; in the face of pointless suffering, belief in a God who could act but does not will appear to some as an insult to human suffering. To confess and proclaim the love of God for a suffering world is not, ultimately, a consolation for all people at all times; nor can it be an epistemological claim about a divine Being who sometimes involves himself in our world. In the end it is only a statement about our own individual experience of the world and of our own lives, and as such, it has no more or less value than other similar statements from any religious perspective or none. In a world of suffering, God may be both a consolation and a stumbling-block, both a solace for the believer and an affront or an irrelevancy to the unbeliever, and it cannot be, nor ever will it be, otherwise.

6

God, History, Contingency

It may be that universal history is the history of the into-nations given a handful of metaphors. (Jorge Luis Borges, 'The Fearful Sphere of Pascal', 1970)

From our standpoint at the beginning of the twenty-first century of the Common Era it is difficult for us to grasp in any real way the power which the idea of God held over Christian society and over the imagination of individual women and men in centuries past. With a few exceptions such as the now quite paganized celebrations of Christmas and Easter, our lives are no longer regulated by the rhythm of the Church's liturgical year. We do not live daily with a powerful imaginative sense of heaven or hell as real locations in which we are likely to spend eternity. Most of us do not think of the world as influenced by powerful unseen forces such as angels, demons, and even Satan, struggling over the future of our immortal souls. The idea of a God who observes us from moment to moment, who watches each sparrow fall to the ground and counts the very hairs on our heads, seems to many in Western society to belong to an age long past.

We are of course well aware that there are still very many fervent believers, often vocal, well-organized and ready to do battle with the unbelievers wherever they are found. But even the believers, for the most part, do not believe in the same way as before. With the exception of some groups with apocalyptic expectations, few Christians expect sudden divine intervention in their lives. They do not anticipate, like the prophets of ancient Israel, a voice from on high which calls on them to do God's will. Nor do they assume that the Lord will control the weather, fight wars on their behalf or raise their friends from the dead. Not many of us would expect God to help us find wives or husbands, and few of us would call for the plague to strike our enemies with any real hope of receiving an answer. Perhaps the divine is to be invoked occasionally in times of trouble or pain, or at times of deep emotion such as birth or death. But as for the daily round of life's ups and downs, it seems that there are few who can still think of the divinity in the same way our ancestors did. God's action in history seems to belong in another time and place.

Even the theology of the Christian churches acknowledges that God does not act now as he once did. In the standard theology of Roman Catholicism, for instance, revelation is past: the great truths about God and humanity have been revealed, and it is now the role of the Church to continue to preach, proclaim, dispense and defend the truth. The deposit of faith as reflected in the doctrines of the early church councils and the language in which they were formulated must be defended from error, for the truth once revealed is the truth for ever.

This way of viewing divine revelation is not confined to Roman Catholicism. The same impulse can be found in those Reformation churches which still cling to biblical literalism in various forms and consider the Hebrew and Christian scriptures to be the very Word of God addressed to humanity. But in this theology the book of the scriptures is closed; it needs no addition, for it contains all that is needed for our salvation. Even in the orthodox theology of the churches God does not seem to act in the way he once did; he now leaves his work up to those who represent him on earth. The *opus dei* or *verbum dei* is now no longer God's own, but is in the hands or mouths of his lieutenants.

Aside from the question of 'official' Christianity's recognition of God's seeming withdrawal from history, we can ask why divine revelation seems consigned to past events, and why any contemporary claims for a theophany would appear so unbelievable to so many people. One answer to that question is that belief in divine intervention in the normal course of everyday events places an impossible burden on the contingencies of history. Once the Western world began to think of 'truth' – whether in the realm of politics, social customs, sexual orientation, race or any other part of life – as produced by historical forces and contexts which themselves contained no inherent objective necessity, then the truth of the dominant religion came itself to be perceived as contingent.

If 'truth' is the product of human history, and if history is contingent, then truth is inescapably contingent also. So, by asking about the contingency of religious truth we are asking about the context and meaning of historical events. These contingent events gave us the 'truth' which we have today, but they could easily have been different.

There are essentially two possible ways to think of this relationship between religious truth and historical contingency. One is to see much of human history, or at least those parts which have a bearing on religious truth, as fully determined by God. In Christian terms the divine plan of salvation works itself out in real historical events (e.g. the life of Jesus of Nazareth). As salvation history is God's plan for humanity, it could not have been different once God decided to act in this way; the truth will out. In its strongest version, in what we could call the predestination model, much Christian theology since Augustine in the fifth century has even regarded the individual's eternal destiny as pre-determined from all time in the mind of God (although many churches have tended to remain mostly silent about this).

The drawback of this view is that it results inevitably in the attenuation, if not the complete elimination, of human freedom. The divine plan of salvation is inexorable and our role is to accept this truth as it has been made known to us. In the theology of those Christian denominations which believe in the doctrine of double predestination, God has destined some of us to salvation and some to damnation, for no particular reason other than the fact that God is God and can therefore do anything he thinks we deserve. As God's will is absolute, this revelation must be accepted in fear and trembling. This fearsome doctrine is simply the logical extrapolation from the perspective that if God is truly God then divine power is absolute. It permits contingency only in the backdrop, in the incidentals of the stage settings; the real drama will unfold as it was meant to be.

This view also raises the question of explaining why a God who plans and controls everything has written into our history so much evil and misery. From this perspective the only answer can be that evil and suffering are to be viewed as the punishment which a wrathful God metes out to unworthy sinners (that is, to all of us). Those Christian theologies which took the theology of predestination seriously could only imagine God as a powerful and fickle ruler, punishing us for the misdemeanour of our forebears Adam and Eve, yet electing to save some of us despite our corrupt nature and let the rest of us go to hell, literally. Not surprisingly, there are relatively few contemporary Christians who hold scrupulously to this view, for it leaves us only with the God of wrath, and this is not a very appealing option when there are other, more enticing possibilities in the spiritual marketplace of contemporary culture.

A less deterministic way of thinking about this is to view most of history as contingent, but to regard some special historical events as due to the direct intervention of God. This is essentially the view of things in the Hebrew Bible: the saving of Noah and his retinue from the flood is God simply deciding to pick this one man as worthy of playing a role in the scheme which he has for the human race; the choosing of Abraham to be the father of a great nation is God's initiative; the subterfuge by which Jacob cheats his brother Esau out of the blessing of their father Isaac seems to be simply part of the plan, as is the escape of Moses and his people from Egypt. Joshua's success in invading the land of Canaan and expunging the indigenous population is aided and abetted by the hand of God. Of course, we now understand a great deal about the formation of the biblical texts and many no longer take these stories as literal descriptions of historical events. We hardly seem to notice that we have also gradually left behind the belief in God's action in history.

A slightly different and less literal emphasis could take the view that history can (mostly) continue on as normal but the true religious meaning in certain events is revealed to those who have eyes to see and ears to hear. This is the approach which the Christian scriptures take to miracles, including the resurrection of Jesus; it is only with the right disposition (nowadays we might say with the correct hermeneutics) that you can see that history has been changed by God. Think of the Ethiopian eunuch in the Acts of the Apostles whom Philip meets on the road through divine intervention. It is only when he has the scriptures explained to him that he can see that Jesus is the one of whom the prophets spoke; without this explanation he would have gone on his way none the wiser of the great miracle which God has worked in Christ (Acts 8.26–40). God has changed the course of human history, but this can only be seen through the eyes of faith.

Such events might cause the sceptic to wonder why God does not intervene more often in the mundane course of events. Why does God choose this occasion rather than that one? Why does God choose to speak to this person and not that person? Why does God choose not to be just a little more clear about what exactly it is that we are to believe and do? In a word, why does God choose not to let more of us in on the truth?

We might also wonder about the relationship between any religion (not just Christianity) which claims to have a special revelation from God and the other religions which make similar claims. If one is true, must not the others, by definition, be deficient if not utterly misleading? And, if the truth is the truth for all, then how is it that relatively so few people know about it? The whole history of Christian mission and evangelization was premised on the idea that the Church bears responsibility for spreading the gospel to all the earth. In the medieval world, where it was assumed that with the exception of Muslims, Jews and a few pagans the whole earth had been evangelized, the Christian Church could afford to be somewhat pleased with its efforts in this regard. Now, at the beginning of the third millennium of Christianity, things look very different, and old-style evangelization is pursued mostly by fundamentalist Protestants and offshoot groups of Christianity, such as the Mormons. It is far easier to change one's theology than to convert the world, so we now hear a great deal about the love of God for all humanity and the eschatological hope that all will be revealed in the end. The conversion of the world has been quietly relocated to the end of time.

The second way to think about the possible relationship between history and religious truth is to admit the real contingency of historical events, including all events once regarded as special acts of divine intervention or revelation. To adopt this position is to admit that had circumstances, personalities or even, on occasion, climatic conditions been different then the 'truth' as we know it would have been different also. The truth claims of Christianity (and the other religions also) have been formed through a succession of indeterminable historical contingencies; everything was not

MONTCALM
COMMUNITY COLLEGE
LIBRARY

determined by divine *fiat*, but what became the truth is dependent upon the contexts and forces which moulded its formation.

Clearly, however, if we take the fact of the sheer contingency of all our religious beliefs seriously, it makes problematic the idea of a God who intervenes in the world from outside to make known to the human race some supernatural truths which are necessary for our salvation. This might seem to some a strange conclusion to reach about the truth of the Christian religion because, after all, is Christianity not about revelation from God? However, consider for one moment what is implied in accepting what has been the dominant view of revelation through most of the past 2,000 years of Christian history.

Allowing for the moment that the true and exclusive revelation of God occurs in the Christian religion, to believe *that* view of divine intervention you have to accept the following. First, God once intervened at will in real human lives to enable us to comprehend his salvific plan, but for a long time now he has, for whatever reason, ceased to do this. Second, God's revelation of the truth to humanity took him approximately 2,000 years from the call of Abraham to the definitive revelation in the cross and resurrection of Jesus Christ. Given that the species *homo sapiens* emerged in Africa perhaps 130,000–160,000 years ago (Tattersall, 1998, p. 173), what was God thinking of in leaving the true revelation as late as he did? (This was the question of the pagan authors Celsus and Porphry to the early Christians: if our salvation was at stake, why did God leave it so late in sending the Saviour?) Third, even if we accept that God's inscrutable will permits him to reveal the truth whenever he so wishes, we must now explain why God chose the particular historical circumstances that he did, some of which, as we have seen in the case of Job, appear reprehensible to human sentiment. Why does Yahweh appear so prone to violence in the Hebrew Bible

MONTCALM
COMMUNITY COLLEGE
LIBRARY

(Old Testament), or why should we automatically assume the
Christian viewpoint that the violent death of Jesus should
show us God's love more clearly than a long life lived in peace
and equanimity with one's family and neighbours (the ideal
in many human cultures)? Why did God choose to reveal the
truth about the meaning of life, death and the universe in
this particular way? And, fourth, if the revelation of God in
Jesus Christ does offer definitive truth about humanity, why
is it plainly so difficult for the majority of human beings (who
are not Christians) to see this? Surely, it should be more
obvious to more people?

As an illustration of the difficulty involved in defending an
interventionist view of divine revelation, we could find no
better example than the turmoil surrounding the fourth-
century disputes on the nature of Jesus of Nazareth, the most
consequential of which was the 'Arian' heresy. It is worthwhile taking a short detour through this historic controversy
to see just how tenuous the 'truth' is, and how close it can
come to being quite a different 'truth' altogether. (In what
follows on the political context of the Arian controversy I am
indebted to Richard E. Rubenstein's captivating study, *When
Jesus Became God: The Struggle to Define Christianity
During the Last Days of Rome* (1999)).

The Arian dispute is such a good example of utter contingency at work because of the simple fact that it was a matter
of political as well as religious chance that the 'orthodoxy' of
the Christian Church came to be what it is. In the early
fourth century, when – to the amazement of Christians and
many others in the ancient world – the Emperor Constantine
first removed the imperial ban on Christianity and then
effectively promoted it as the favoured religion of the Empire,
there was much that remained to be decided about what
exactly it was that Christians were expected to believe. From
Constantine's point of view a unified Empire could greatly
benefit from a unified religion, and it was better to resolve

doctrinal matters than to have Christians from different parts of the Empire squabbling about what to believe and what not to believe. For that reason the Emperor took a keen interest in theology and there was no more pressing theological question than the issue of the divinity of Jesus.

Unlike in our present age, when the idea of a god-man is more difficult for many to envisage, few fourth-century Christians doubted that Jesus Christ was a divine being. The really pressing question was: is Jesus' divine status equal to or less than that of God the Father? This question was perfectly intelligible in a cultural and religious context in which divine beings, like humans, could have different levels of importance. The Greeks worshipped Zeus as supreme among the Greek pantheon, but he was not the only deity, and it was natural for the ordinary person to think in terms of an order of divinities; while respecting Zeus, one could quite freely make an offering to Isis, Mithras or Apollo.

Christianity did not emerge out of ancient Palestine with its doctrine already pre-formed; it had to be worked out within a pagan context of a plurality of divinities; understanding this enables us to comprehend one of the most fascinating aspects of the Arian controversy: the engagement of the ordinary Christian in this apparently abstruse theological dispute. Arius – a priest from the North African port city of Alexandria – wrote popular songs defending his position that Jesus was divine but could not be considered the equal of God the Father, and these songs became popular among the sailors and dock-workers of the Mediterranean. Arianism was a quarrel which concerned everyone, for it involved the belief system which the religion favoured by the Emperor himself would embrace; it was a struggle for the soul of the Empire. Everyone was interested in God, for how could you not be?

Arius' chief opponent was Athanasius (d. 373 CE), the future hero of Christian orthodoxy, who was first a deacon in

Alexandria and later the bishop there. Athanasius' view was that Jesus and God the Father were one and that the Arian theology was virtually a lapse back into the pagan pluralism of divinities or, when taken further, could result in Christ being perceived as merely mortal, as the Jews and pagans thought. What makes Athanasius' ultimate victory fascinating is that throughout much of the fourth century a majority of Christian bishops, especially in the eastern part of the Empire where Christianity was strongest, were Arians who, despite their internal differences, all rejected the principle that Christ could be considered equal to God the Father.

Subsequent Christian doctrinal theology has generally argued that the orthodox position declared at the Council of Nicea in 325 was by necessity the correct one, chiefly on the grounds that Arianism – with its concept of Christ as a divine being who was something less than the fullness of God – could not achieve the salvation promised by the doctrine of God's very self becoming a human being in the incarnation. Yet doctrines alone seldom win over emperors and empires, and the manner of how Athanasius' view finally won out presents a set of sobering questions for anyone who would wish to defend the interventionist view that God reveals the truth in and through the mundane events of history.

The Arian dispute was no mere bookish squabble between dry-as-dust theologians: it involved imperial power at the highest level, impacted upon the lives of everyone who took sides in the dispute, and concerned the belief system of the greater part of the known world at the time. It was as public an issue as a modern-day presidential election and went on for well over half a century. The character and the behaviour of the main players was as much a part of the issue as the doctrinal dispute itself, and in the case of Athanasius in particular, his ruthless methods very nearly became the undoing not only of himself but of the whole 'orthodox' position.

Athanasius was a remarkable man by any standards.

Through sheer physical stamina, dogged belief in his own opinion, indefatigable effort, considerable political skill and no little ruthlessness towards his opponents, he almost single-handedly kept the 'orthodox' position alive when Arianism was in the ascendant across the Empire. Yet in the course of the violent disputes which swung first one way and then the other for decades, this future hero of Christian orthodoxy was accused by his fellow bishops of organizing violent repression of recalcitrant clergy (including the severe beating of at least one Arian bishop), was berated personally by Constantine for his intemperance, and effectively accused of treason in front of the Emperor by Bishop Eusebius of Nicomedia (the bishop accused Athanasius of plotting to cut off the supply of grain to the main cities of the Empire by using his influence in Alexandria to blockade the port). Encountering the personal wrath of Constantine, he was excommunicated by the Council of Tyre in 335 and exiled to the German town of Trier, lucky to escape with his life.

In the meantime, during Athanasius' exile, Arius, having himself been exiled and condemned on several previous occasions, had his views declared orthodox by the Emperor and several councils of bishops. The Council of Constantinople in 336, with the agreement of the Emperor, gave him permission to reclaim his church in Alexandria, but he dropped dead in Constantinople on the very night before he was due to be re-admitted publicly to full communion with the church. Arius' sudden death is one of the great ironies of Christian history and was the occasion of much glee on the part of Athanasius, who saw in it divine vindication of his own views. Then, when Constantine himself died the following year (337), Athanasius was free to resume his political and religious agitation throughout the Empire, eventually returning to his power base in Alexandria to lead the anti-Arian campaign.

After the death of Constantine, the struggle for control of the Empire resulted in his pro-Arian son Constantius coming to power. The new Emperor sought unity and agreement from a moderate Arian position, and in 357 the Second Council of Sirmium drafted a creed which for the first time introduced Arianism into official Christian orthodoxy. This council banned the Nicene term *homoousion* (of one essence), and reasoned sensibly that knowledge of the essence of God is beyond human comprehension (Rubenstein, 1999, pp. 186–7). In 359 an Arian creed was agreed (under intense political pressure) at Rimini in the west and Seleucia in the east, and the Christian Church had Arianism as its official doctrine. But the very following year, the pro-Arian Emperor Constantius died of natural causes and the imperial throne passed to his nephew, the famous Julian, known to Christians as 'the Apostate'. Julian, to everyone's surprise, turned out to have been harbouring secret pagan views, and he soon set about limiting the influence of Christianity and restoring the old mystery religions to their former dominant role. During this upheaval, violence broke out across the Empire and the Arian Bishop of Alexandria was murdered by a mob of pagans and pro-Nicene Christians.

In the long term, however, Julian's apostasy did not break apart the Christian community but brought it closer together in common cause, and when he died in battle against the Persians in 363 he was eventually succeeded by the pro-Arian Valens. Valens, however, was killed by Visigoths at Hadrianopolis in 378 – a catastrophic event in Roman history – and was succeeded by Theodosius, a pro-Nicene confidant of Bishop Ambrose of Milan. Under Theodosius the anti-Arian position was strengthened, and the Council of Constantinople in 381 sealed the theology of Nicea as Christian orthodoxy.

While the Nicene view supported by Athanasius eventually triumphed because the imperial pendulum swung the Nicene way, it is also the case that Christian theologians found ways of explaining how Jesus could be fully one with

God and yet not absorbed totally into the identity of the Father. Many conservative Arians (those who believed that Jesus was similar in essence to the Father, although not equal to him) found that they had more in common with Nicene Christians than they did with the radical Arians (who saw Christ as a creature dissimilar from God). In the end, the Arians could not find enough common ground between themselves. Notwithstanding the Arians' failure, however, theological solutions without political influence are rarely successful, and the 'orthodoxy' we have today is inseparable from the fortunes of fourth-century imperial politics.

So much for the vicissitudes of history. If Arius had lived, would the Christian doctrine of God have been different? If Athanasius had died in exile in the cold north-west of the Empire, would the Arian view have won out comfortably? Or, if Constantine, despite his age, had lived to keep Athanasius in exile for longer, would Arianism have become so entrenched as to become impossible to extirpate? If either Constantius or Valens had lived longer, would Arianism have triumphed? Most interestingly, if the young Julian had lived, would paganism have regained the ground it had lost to Christianity? (The answer to this latter question is 'Probably not', as Christianity was by that time firmly entrenched in the Greco-Roman world.)

We can only speculate about other possible directions which Christian belief could have taken. The eventual victory of what came to be called 'orthodoxy' does not take away from the fact that it was a very close-run thing; had some of the significant factors been slightly different then the Arians could have won out, and Christianity – at least in terms of its core belief system – would have become a quite different religion.

The Arian controversy offers just one instance (among many possible candidates) of how one central aspect of Christian belief is inseparable from the mundane circumstances of social, political and cultural history. Of course Christian theologians have not been unaware of this issue, and in accounting for the eventual triumph of 'orthodoxy', Christianity has traditionally appealed to the workings of God the Holy Spirit in guiding the Church towards doctrinal truth. But if doctrine is understood as revealed by the action of God, then the Holy Spirit must have taken a very close interest in battle tactics and imperial politics, for it was a very long and tortuous road to 'orthodoxy'.

To believe in the direct guidance of the Holy Spirit in this manner involves accepting that God works by intervening in the course of history in very precise ways. Can we actually believe that God so arranged it that Constantine became Emperor through winning the famous battle at the Milvian Bridge, or that divine guidance arranged Athanasius' trials and near-failure before final success, or that the death of Arius at an opportune moment for the Athanasian party was caused by God striking him down to ensure the success of orthodoxy? If we cannot accept these events as caused by direct divine intervention, then how was God operating through these individuals and these events? We could respond by appealing to the effect of divine grace, but this leaves us with another series of difficult questions. Were Arius and his followers completely bereft of divine guidance, given that they were not completely unorthodox in *all* their beliefs? Or, how precisely was God's grace manifest in Constantine's battle to become Emperor or his decision to become a Christian? Was Athanasius guided by divine grace only when thinking about doctrine but not when he encouraged violence against his Arian opponents?

In the end, did it really matter to God whether the appellation *homoousios* ('of the same being') was applied to Jesus' relation to the Father rather than *homoiousios* ('of similar being'), one small letter making all the difference between truth and heresy? Was this belief (or its converse) worth one

life? Yet from the viewpoint of Christian orthodoxy, which
believes that the doctrines of Christianity are God's revelation, it is necessary to insist that somehow God was
intervening in the historical process which led to these views
being accepted as the true doctrines of the Church. But can
Christians today still stand by Bishop Ambrose of Milan's
view that the slaughter of the Roman army by the Visigoths
at Hadrianopolis was God's act of judgement on the Arians?
Hardly. If we accept the real contingency of historical events
then we have to accept that direct divine intervention was
absent from the whole process and that Christian orthodoxy
might well have been different. Either God intervened in a
way that seems impossible for most modern educated people
to accept, or the events of the time were due to the efforts of
the participants and nothing else.

To put this another way: to believe in the intervention of
God in historical events in order to influence their outcome in
a particular theological direction raises questions about
God's nature, actions and intentions. If God intervenes like a
capricious and meddling human being attempting to get his
own way, then what sort of God is this? And if God does intervene, why did he not intervene more effectively and
decisively to influence more of the fourth-century bishops at
an earlier date and save the Christian Church much death,
pain and misery? The conclusion we must draw is that the
idea of a God who interferes, manipulates, adjusts and
fashions human affairs to achieve a particular desired
outcome results is an impossible chimera of a God, an elusive,
shifting, capricious, equivocal character who intervenes or is
absent when it suits.

But we have no knowledge when these divine interven-
tions might occur, so must we then rely upon some other
authority to tell us how and when God intervenes? In this
respect the flight of Western Christianity to the security of
authority, either in its Roman Catholic form of papal infal-

libility or its Protestant form of literal divine inspiration of the Bible, can be seen as an attempt to keep history at bay, to rebuff the possibility that what becomes religious truth is the result not of divine intervention but of human religious searching and not a little power and politics. The belief that what became Christian orthodoxy is precisely what God wanted us to believe impelled great Christian missionary drives in conjunction with colonial expansion, and resulted in quite a lot of blood being shed in the name of truth.

God, in this powerful picture of expansionist Christianity, gives us a truth *in* history which is not *of* history; like Plato's forms it is a universal truth which cannot be changed in any way by human activity. Like Christ it is the same yesterday, today and for ever because it was given to us by God's own revelation. Yet, as we have seen, believing in that truth involves believing in divine intervention in real historical events, in real arguments, wars, quibbles over Greek philosophical terms, and in real lives and deaths.

In a world where belief in the miraculous was commonplace and the presence of the gods in human affairs taken for granted, the power of mysterious forces over the everyday was less difficult to comprehend than it is for us today. Yet what are we to make of this? Either God is capricious, whimsical and not a little unclear about what is expected of us, or else God does not interfere from behind the scenes to get his way in theological disputes. In short, to believe in the interventionist God is to cease to have confidence in history as the product of our own efforts, and either we accept that the contingency of all history, including the history of religious doctrines, goes all the way down the line or it does not. If it does go all the way down then we have to look for a God who is not merely a projection of our own attitudes and actions, fear, hope, hate and love. There is, to paraphrase Lessing, an unbridgeable chasm between history and revelation as it has been traditionally understood.

Does all of this mean that we can never know religious truth? The answer to this depends on what we mean by religious 'truth'. If we mean an eternal and unchanging doctrine guaranteed by biblical or ecclesiastical authority, then as historical, finite beings we can never know that. If we mean a searching after a possibility that may be real, an attempt to express our own deepest experiences of reality within a framework where 'God' is the central, focal symbol, then it is of course possible for us to know religious truth, for it is our own truth of our own making. But all religious searching after 'God' takes place in an epistemological context where certainty is absent and knowledge of the divine is always deferred because it is unachievable.

The greatest of the theologians and mystics were aware of this inability of the human ever to reach certainty about God, and they attributed this to a combination of human frailty and the depths of the divine mystery. However, today, any theology which emphasizes the inadequacy of the human mind to fasten on to the nature of God does so within a cultural context where we also must acknowledge that it is quite possible that no such divine reality exists. Even allowing for the distinction which the Christian tradition at its best made between God-as-such, the divine mystery in itself, and our words about God (including the doctrine of the Trinity) we can no longer accept that our language ever escapes the historically contingent conditions from which it emerged.

Now aware of the historical conditioning attending all religious formulations and beliefs, we are challenged to move beyond the boundaries of the self-enclosed cultural enclaves which have been part and parcel of our religious heritage for millennia. All religions, including those which think of themselves as bearers of the single truth, are local, contingent and relative; they are the products of human history. The challenge we face is whether we are capable of encountering the

richness of our great religious traditions creatively, imaginatively and with respect, rather than either rejecting them as
leftovers from an age of ignorance or, conversely, treating
them as absolute vehicles of divine truth.

At the very least, recognizing the sheer inadequacy of all
religious talk to escape the contingency of history should
make us aware that all religious beliefs (doctrines, prayers,
scriptures, etc.) have an air of unreality about them, that they
are in the end, to paraphrase Aquinas, words of straw. At the
most, this recognition could lead us to base our religious
activities on hope, not on certainty; on respect, not on religious rivalry; on mutual recognition of the accidental nature
of all our 'truth' rather than on condemnation of those who
are different.

When the sheer contingency of all religious belief is
acknowledged then the boundaries between religions and
between groups within religions begin to break down. What
great truth about human life does the Muslim have that the
Christian does not? What secret knowledge does the Christian possess that the Jew, Buddhist or Hindu cannot? What
does the orthodox believer have that the 'heretic' does not? Of
course there are significant empirical difference between and
within the beliefs, rituals, customs and symbolism of each
great religious tradition, but recognizing this truism does not
give us knowledge of some 'extra' criterion which would
enable us to make a final judgement about where the 'truth'
could lie.

There is no vantage point outside of history which would
enable us to claim that this event or that one is the clear revelation of God for all people at all times. Even our most sacred
traditions should stand under this criterion. Those of us who
call ourselves Christians must remember that while some
first-century Jews saw in the cross of Jesus the ultimate revelation of God, other Jews saw only the sad but unremarkable
spectacle of another innocent victim of Imperial Rome.

According to Paul, Jesus' cross was a stumbling-block for the Jews, and foolishness to the Greeks (1 Corinthians 1.23), and this is as true now as it was then. But this time there is no need to imply blame, for history tells us that there are no unambiguous revelations, no clear messages from the beyond. Above all, it tells us that there is no room for the arrogant sense of superiority which has been so characteristic of Christianity over much of the past 2,000 years.

What of Christian truth then? What about the privileged claims of the revelation of God the Father, his Son Jesus Christ, and his outpouring in the Holy Spirit? Van A. Harvey, in his influential study *The Historian and the Believer,* put it like this:

> The situation is not so much that the Christian has access to realities to which the non-Christian does not, or that the Christian believes that certain entities exist which the non-Christian finds doubtful. The situation is, rather, that both Christian and non-Christian are confronted with the same realities but interpret them differently. They regard them from different perspectives. (Harvey, 1996, p. 284)

The Christian doctrine of the Trinity, over which so much ink has been spilled and so many lives lost, is nothing more than the faltering attempt of one community to describe its encounter with the divine. It is the working out in history of this people's understanding of their experience, saying: 'This is how *we* encounter the ultimate, this is how *we* understand God.' If others find these doctrines impossible to accept or even to begin to understand, little is lost. In religion, truth is in the eye of the beholder.

This recognition of the historical contingency of all religious beliefs and truth-claims, does not mean that we should advocate a relativistic view of all human meanings and cultural practices. Ethical criteria still apply. Using *sharia* law to justify the whipping of a 14-year-old girl is still immoral. The institutional misogyny of Roman Catholicism cannot justify itself by making claims on God's will. White supremacism masquerading as Protestant piety abuses the religious message of the New Testament. Racist nationalism which takes on the guise of a Hindu revival is abhorrent. And so also is the apartheid which hides behind biblical claims to territorial control of the land of Palestine.

To think of religious truth as historically contingent is to reject all absolutisms, but it is not to condone relativism. It is simply to regard all religious belief as ours, as human, and not as a revelation from outside our world. Perhaps there is a divine being who made us and cared for us, or perhaps not; we can only react to the world as it appears to us and no more, but in so doing we can never be justified in thinking that the truth is ours alone. To continue to claim that the accidents of history which have given rise to our religious beliefs have given us the truth for all peoples, times and places is to mistake the image for the reality, the finite for the infinite. History tells us that our religious truth is, in the end, only the intonations we give to a handful of metaphors.

7

God and the Cosmos

In this materialistic age of ours the serious scientific workers are the only profoundly religious people. (Albert Einstein, *The World as I See It*, 1935)

This small planet on which we live orbits a medium-sized star in one of at least half a billion (500 million) galaxies in the known (visible) universe. In a typical galaxy there are approximately 10 billion stars. The universe itself is about 15 billion years old and has expanded outwards from a tiny point, or singularity, of fantastic density to form the stars and planets as we know them. The universe which we know (there may well be many others) continues to expand outwards from its original singularity and, following the second law of thermodynamics, it is expected by many scientists to end in thermodynamic equilibrium, that is, in heat-death. If this happens then there will be left only a cold and relatively inanimate universe in which there are no more star formations, no more burning gases or other chemical reactions, just the lifeless remnant of what was once the whole of material reality as we know it. Alternatively, some scientists think that the universe may contract onto itself under the force of gravity and result in a 'big crunch'. Either way the universe as we know it will not last for ever.

Our Sun, thankfully still full of life, formed about 4.5 billion years ago, the debris emitted during its formation cooling to give rise to the planets and moons in our solar system. It is estimated that the Sun has somewhat over half of its life left to run, after which its supply of hydrogen will be exhausted and it will burn up in an expanding fireball which will encompass the earth and destroy whatever life may be left here.

If the enormity of this universe astounds us, we can be even more astonished when we encounter the strange nature of the quantum world. With the splitting of the atom in the first half of the last century came insights which showed us the world as we could never have imagined it before. At the sub-atomic level the 'normal' laws of Newtonian physics no longer apply. Heisenberg's Uncertainty Principle (after the physicist Werner Heisenberg) stipulates that it is not possible to measure accurately both the position and momentum of an electron or other sub-atomic particle; if you know where it is you do not know how fast it is moving and if you know how fast it is moving you cannot determine precisely where it is.

Furthermore, it appears that the quantum world is one in which the presence of an observer at an experiment appears to influence the behaviour of electrons and other particles, although some scientists hold the view that at the quantum level entities simply do not have the properties we tend to expect and that observation simply acts to realize one of many potentialities (see Barbour, 2000, Chapter 3). Either way, while scientists differ on whether this feature of the quantum world is due to human limitation or to inherent qualities in these entities themselves, what is certain is that there is an indeterminacy at the quantum level which is nothing like the behaviour of objects in the macro level explained by Newtonian physics. Sub-atomic particles do not behave like aeroplanes, trains or falling leaves. When we think of the composition of matter in the world as we know it – filled with rocks, tables, bodies and other firm objects – and think that the atoms which go to make them up themselves comprise mostly empty space, we are truly at the limits of our normal conceptual categories. As the physicist and theologian Ian Barbour comments, 'the quantum atom is inaccessible to direct observation and unimaginable in terms of everyday properties; it cannot even be coherently described in terms of classical physical concepts such as space, time, and causality' (p. 67).

All of this is so staggering that it is difficult for the human mind to comprehend. What can it all mean, if it 'means' anything at all? Did the universe just somehow 'happen', or was it designed by an intelligence infinitely greater than anything you or I can comprehend? Is there some purpose in all this vastness or is it simply the effect of the inexorable laws of physics working themselves out over vast periods of time? When we think about it, why are there *laws* of physics at all? Why not simply random events, with no structure or reliability? Why, in the end, is there something rather than nothing? In recent years, these and related questions have led to a renewed interest by theologians and scientists alike in the question of whether the universe shows evidence of intelligent design; whether, perhaps, behind it all there might be a God who has created it with just the right conditions to allow life to emerge.

In his influential book, *The First Three Minutes: A Modern View of the Origin of the Universe* (1977), Steven Weinberg describes the aftermath of the Big Bang:

At the end of the first three minutes the contents of the universe were mostly in the form of light, neutrinos and anti-neutrinos . . . This matter continued to rush apart, becoming steadily cooler and less dense. Much later, after a few hundred thousand years, it would become cool enough for electrons to join with nuclei to form atoms of hydrogen and helium. The resulting gas would

begin under the influence of gravitation to form clumps,
which would ultimately condense to form the galaxies
and stars of the present universe. However, the ingredi-
ents with which the stars would begin their life would
be just those prepared in the first three minutes.
(Weinberg, in Danielson, 2000, p. 436)

In this remarkable process the most remarkable fact of all is
that it occurred in this precise manner and with these exact
physical characteristics. The most astonishing thing about
the universe is that it has the physical properties which it
has, properties which permitted atoms and molecules to come
about, which allowed galaxies, stars and planets to form and,
eventually, life to emerge. At the moment of the Big Bang and
just after, precisely the right conditions had to occur in order
for the universe as we know it to come about. In order for
galaxies to form, gases had to be distributed evenly and to
have precisely the right temperature for oxygen to form. If
the balances had been slightly different, then stars might
have burned themselves out very quickly indeed and would
not have lasted for the billions of years which (in our case at
least) allowed a planet to form which eventually gave rise to
life. Too little energy and the universe would have contracted
on itself; too much energy and its elements would have dissi-
pated without stars and galaxies forming. It had to be just so.
We can, without too much difficulty, imagine a universe of
torpid gases or dead matter, simply there with no nuclear
reactions and no chemical activity. Such a universe would be
arid and lifeless.

Writing in the journal *Nature* back in 1931, the physicist
Sir Arthur Stanley Eddington estimated the chances of a
universe such as ours coming into existence at random as
being of the order of 'multillions' to one (a multillion being
number of the order 10^{10} billion or greater), an incredible
number. Much more recently, the cosmologist Lee Smolin

estimates that the possibility of there being a universe which contains stars at all stands at about 10^{229} to 1 (Smolin, in Danielson, 2000, p. 473), which still seems a very low probability when expressed in this way. Also remarkable is the fact that Newton's gravitational constant (which permits us to calculate the gravitational force acting between any two bodies) is an astonishingly small number (described by Smolin as 'a ridiculous number': 10^{-38} as measured between protons). Yet without this very weak gravitational force the universe would not be as we know it today. It is the very weakness of the gravitational constant which requires more and more protons to come together before the pressure in the potential star is great enough to begin a nuclear reaction. If the gravitational force were stronger we would have had reactions which burned themselves out very quickly, and we would not have the long burning stars of which our Sun is one.

Smolin points out other equally astonishing qualities of our universe, for example the remarkably delicate balance in the masses of the elementary particles (such as protons, neutrons and electrons) which allow nuclei to form and atoms to remain stable. Without this precise balance the material world as we know it could not have come into being. Without the weakness of the cosmological constant (a number which describes the mass of empty space, a counter intuitive concept but one allowed for in Einstein's general theory of relativity), which stands at 10^{-40} in units of proton mass, matter would be unable to resist the power of this force and the universe could collapse in on itself. Again there would be no stars, no planets and no life.

Smolin goes on to explain that if any of the four basic forces in the universe (gravity, electromagnetism and the strong and weak nuclear forces) were to be either changed in its range or its strength, or even were to be eliminated completely, then 'the universe around us will evaporate instantly and a vastly different world will come into being' (Smolin [1997], in Danielson, 2000, p. 472). He wants us to think of the probability of a universe which allows for just the precise balance of the four forces, as well as that of the elementary particles and the interaction between the two: is it merely chance that this combination could come into being and produce the world as we know it? Is the possibility of a universe calculated at 10^{229} to 1 really only the outcome of blind chance, or is there some other answer? Of course if we follow Smolin's guidance here we have to acknowledge that the possibility of *any* particular individual universe existing is equally improbable, but what makes this one interesting is not simply the fact that for us it is the only one that we have, but rather that we humans, self-conscious and intelligent beings, are here to think about it. This, as we shall see, has raised some interesting questions about what *our* significance in such a universe might be.

Smolin offers three possibilities to account for the universe being as it is. First, belief in a God who created the universe so that beings could arise who were capable of responding to this God. He dismisses this as a mystical answer which would make science dependent on faith. Second, the possibility that there is only one way for the universe to be and for this way to be described by a single mathematical theory. No such theory has yet been found, but if it were we would have to believe that our universe had been given to us by a mathematical possibility of 1 in 10^{229}; this surely, he thinks, would turn us all into mystics, for if there were only one way for the world to be then even God would have no option but to create it. Third, he speculates that the parameters of the universe as we know it may change in time and that therefore new physical configurations may come into being, giving rise to new but for us unattainable universes.

He goes on to speculate that there could be multiple universes which could come into being in black holes, and current thinking in cosmology considers this at least a reasonable possibility. Cosmologists seem right now to concur that if there are multiple universes there is no causal connection between them. So if there are other universes it is unlikely that we shall ever experience them; this universe is all that *we* have. We shall have to leave the question of what is inside a black hole to those more competent to deal with it.

What, then, are we to make of the first of Smolin's three possibilities, that this unlikely universe was created by a deity? The most obvious response, having seen the sheer improbability of this universe being as it is, is that theism is the simplest, most parsimonious, explanation. Surely, the easiest way to explain the universe is to say that it was created by a super-intelligence who gave it just the right parameters to enable stars and planets to form and life to eventually emerge. Yet Eddington, Smolin and many other physicists and cosmologists are not willing to countenance the possibility of design, and this view is comprehensible at least on the grounds that any deity that might exist is always going to be beyond the bounds of experimental physics. God, quite literally, cannot be brought into the equation. Yet, the sheer improbability of the universe as we know it existing issues a challenge to physics and cosmology to explain why it is *just so*, and it is not surprising that scientists continue to disagree on the issue.

One way to read the theistic hypothesis is according to the so-called *anthropic principle* (from the Greek for 'man', *anthropos*). We humans, intelligent life forms, are here in the universe. Out of the range of possible universes which there could have been, the possibilities for the existence of one which could sustain life are, as we have seen, very small indeed. The anthropic principle argues that the sheer improbability of the universe having the precise properties suitable for the emergence of life, especially intelligent life, means that the universe must have been designed so that such intelligent life could emerge. After all, not only do the laws of physics have to be exactly the way they are but the conditions on this planet (and, perhaps, on other planets in the universe) have to be a certain way in order to permit life to flourish; any old planet will not do, as we can see in the case of our neighbours in this solar system. The distance of the earth from the Sun, being neither too close nor too far away, the stability of the earth's rotation around the Sun (thus giving rise to seasons), the variability yet regularity of earth's climate, the constancy of our atmosphere, the abundance of water and other factors, make the fact that we are here seem to be beyond the bounds of mere chance. Surely, out of all the myriad possibilities for universes that could have been, the fact that the universe that we have is one which would allow us to be here is too much to ascribe to contingency? (See Barrow and Tipler (1986) for the full argument.)

In similar vein, the historian of science Owen Gingrich points to the extraordinarily fortuitous fact (for us, a carbon-based life form) that carbon atoms could form at all. The atomic make-up of both carbon and oxygen is such that if the atomic resonance of the oxygen nucleus was less than one-half of one per cent higher, then all the carbon in the universe would have been converted to oxygen. Without this fine-tuning, carbon would be rare in the universe, and without carbon we would not be here. Gingrich, himself a Christian, draws the conclusion that 'a common sense and satisfying interpretation of our world suggests the designing hand of a superintelligence' (Gingrich, in Danielson, 2000, p. 526).

However, following the other possible interpretation of the improbability of our universe, John Leslie argues that 'the fine tuning [of the fundamental laws of physics] is evidence of the following fact: *that God is real, and/or there are many and varied universes*' (Leslie, 1989, p. 198). Leslie's preference is for the latter option, and perhaps, following Smolin's calculation, we can speculate that there might be as many as 10^{229} universes, at least one of which is suitable for the emergence of intelligent life. However, even if we can agree in theory that other universes might exist, it does not help us very much in deciding whether this one is designed or came about by mere chance; arguing over the balance of probabilities does not help us draw any firm conclusions. What we do know is we have at least one universe and, improbable as it might be in statistical terms, it is one which has the right conditions for intelligent life to come about.

So, while we may entertain the imaginative possibility that there are multiple universes, it seems to remain at least a plausible hypothesis that this universe is the way it is because it has been designed this way. This is the basic starting-point of those who promote a theistic explanation. Speaking of the mathematical beauty of the physical laws of the universe, theologian Keith Ward argues that the appropriate response to the improbability of the universe being the way it is, is to consider first of all any postulate that would make it more probable. For Ward,

> [t]he postulate that raises its probability to the highest degree is the postulate that some mind . . . intends to bring into existence a physical realm which actualizes a subset of elegant possibilities. That would explain with complete adequacy the extraordinary precision of the Big Bang that began this universe. (Ward, 1996, p. 46)

Ward's target here is partly the view that the universe could have emerged out of nothing due to quantum fluctuations, what cosmologist Alan Guth has called the 'ultimate free lunch' (see Guth, 1997).

This form of the argument for theism ultimately rests on the question of the improbability of this universe existing with the precise physical laws and conditions which it has. It also operates from the principle that the most simple explanation is to be preferred to more complex explanations or to no explanation at all; in this case the most simple explanation is to postulate the existence of God. So, reading the scientific evidence in this way allows us to think of the possibility of the universe being the creation of God.

However, not everyone reads the evidence in this way. Steven Weinberg is a good example of a scientist who does not see the theistic explanation as plausible. Weinberg takes issue with the basic idea behind the anthropic principle, namely, that the improbability of the universe being the way it is means that the universe shows evidence of design:

> You don't have to invoke a benevolent designer to explain why we are in one of the parts of the universe where life is possible: in all other parts of the universe there is no one to raise the question. If any theory of this general type [i.e. given that the cosmological constant – i.e. the energy density of empty space – could be any value, the theory that there are many big bangs with varying cosmological constants, some of which favor conditions suitable for the emergence of life and the majority of which do not] turns out to be correct, then to conclude that the constants of nature have been fine-tuned by a benevolent designer would be like saying, 'Isn't it wonderful that God put us here on earth, where there's water and air and the surface gravity and temperature are so comfortable, rather than some horrid place, like Mercury or Pluto?' Where else in the solar system other than earth could we have evolved? (Weinberg, 1999, p. 47)

Weinberg defends the possibility of there being multiple universes in which the physical constants take different values and that the universe which we know is simply the result of one such possibility being actualized. He regards the anthropic principle as simply 'mumbo jumbo'; if there are a large number of universes then the fact that one of them gave rise to life is simply the luck of the draw. However, even if we did admit that there were other worlds, we would still have to speculate on the probability of one of them having the physical characteristics liable to give rise to life, some of it intelligent. How we would go about doing this adequately, if at all, stretches the bounds of imagination, for we would have to acknowledge that the existence of *any* universe having *any* particular set of characteristics was equally improbable. This also simply pushes the question of a Creator back one step; why should we not just as easily speculate that there are many worlds in which life can emerge and that these worlds are also the work of a divine Being?

The only conclusion we can draw is that it is not legitimate to infer either the 'existence' or 'non-existence' of God from the probability of this or any other universes existing. Belief in a transcendent creator God may be a satisfying explanation for the beauty and magnificence of the universe, but it is not something which can be inferred from the evidence adduced by modern physics and cosmology. We are left, in the end, with the possibility of reading the universe in different ways. The theistic explanation may be the simplest, but it is not at all self-evident and the evidence which the universe offers us remains ambivalent. So for anyone who finds the theistic explanation most convincing, it is important to realize that the new arguments for theism based on the improbability of this universe being as it is are not new versions of the old natural theology which tried to prove the existence of God. In the twelfth century Thomas Aquinas argued, following Aristotle, that we could not have an infinite regress of causes and that we were therefore compelled to assume the existence of a First Cause which, as Aquinas puts it, everyone calls 'God'. In the nineteenth century William

Paley famously argued that if you found a watch on the ground you would assume from its complex construction the existence of a watchmaker; by analogy, when we look at this world and the universe as a whole in its beauty and complexity we are led to assume the existence of a Designer.

Yet neither of these arguments, or others like them, can be considered convincing as 'proofs'. As we have seen, many scientists think that the laws of physics may simply be the product of chance, as improbable as that might seem. Against the idea of an uncaused cause, David Hume, in the eighteenth century, maintained that we could not legitimately infer an originating cause from a series of finite events; we cannot move logically from the finite to the infinite. The arguments which we meet among present-day theologians interested in these questions do not for the most part attempt to demonstrate God's existence on the basis of the scientific evidence or prove that the theistic explanation is the only viable one (for an exception see Stannard, 2000). Rather, they argue in terms of what they see as the high probability of theism, its simplicity as an explanation and its coherence with other factors such as religious experience. But the universe itself offers us no unequivocal answer. In the words of John Hick: 'If the question is whether from all this we can validly infer God, the answer has to be No. But if the question is whether, from a religious standpoint, the universe can properly be seen as a creation or emanation or expression of the divine, the answer has to be Yes' (Hick, 1989, p. 85).

If some form of religious explanation for our universe is at least plausible then we can legitimately ask questions about how a possible divine creator might relate to the creation. Yet it must also be openly acknowledged that thinking in terms of a divine cause of the universe does not bring us anywhere close to belief in a personal God, but rather allows us only to think in terms of a God more like the Great Architect of the seventeenth- and eighteenth-century Deists, a God who made the world in all its glory yet allows it to continue on its own way, governed by the laws established at the original creation. In the seventeenth and eighteenth centuries, this concept of God was very appealing to many intellectuals who were disillusioned by the religious wars in Europe, dissatisfied by what they saw as the bickering over obscure points of doctrine, and distrustful of claims of special revelation. It remains an attractive option for anyone who wishes to posit a divine origin of the world, and it is, I suspect, more common in Western society than might be expected. But Deism, however intellectually satisfying as an explanation of the cause of things, offers little more than this. The Deist God is not a God to pray to or become angry at; it is not a God who cares about you and me and may not even be a God who cares much about the creation (see Byrne, 1997, Chapter 5).

Another way to view the God–world relation is pantheism (from the Greek for 'all' and 'god'), although this idea really subverts the concept of a relation by reducing God to the world. While forms of pantheism existed in both ancient Indian and Western thought, modern pantheism dates from the seventeenth-century philosopher Baruch Spinoza. Spinoza's logical system in philosophy led him to think of God as a necessary existing Being, yet he could not reconcile this idea with the idea of a contingent world. What followed was his severe critique of the classical theistic idea of a God who exists external to the world; for Spinoza we cannot think of the world as external to a necessary existing being, God. We must, therefore, think of the universe itself as a unity, comprising the relation God–World in one reality. God or nature, they are the same. Spinoza's pantheism questioned the assumption that there could exist an unproblematic cause–effect relation between God and the world: an infinite immaterial being causing a finite material world. But Spinoza argued that if God is not physical then we cannot trace the physical world back to God, so we must think of the necessary existing being, God, as physical. We must think of God and the world as one (see Hartshorne and Reese, 2000, p. 190).

Spinoza's pantheism greatly influenced the religious views of Albert Einstein. Einstein, too, could not think of a God who existed externally to the world. The idea of a personal God who interacted with the creation made no sense to him. For Einstein the anthropomorphic idea of a God of providence 'who protects, disposes, rewards and punishes' is simply the product of primitive fear. What matters is what he called 'cosmic religious feeling' in which an individual person 'feels the nothingness of human desires and aims and the sublimity and marvellous order which reveal themselves both in nature and in the world of thought' (Einstein, 1935, p. 24). For Einstein, the idea of a personal God acting in the world and overseeing our moral choices is impossible:

> I cannot conceive of a personal God who would directly influence the actions of individuals, or would directly sit in judgment on creatures of his own creation. I cannot do this in spite of the fact that mechanistic causality has, to a certain extent, been placed in doubt by modern science [i.e., by quantum physics]. My religiosity consists in a humble admiration of the infinitely superior spirit that reveals itself in the little that we, with our weak and transitory understanding, can comprehend of reality. Morality is of the highest importance – but for us, not for God. (Einstein, in Dukas and Hoffman, 1979, p. 66)

Pantheism challenges the idea of a personal God by destroying the notion of God's transcendence which was an essential part of classical theism. If God is reduced to the world, then all talk of God's 'relation' to the world becomes

meaningless. What happens in the world happens to God, and
there is no room for providence or divine influence on the
course of natural events.

In the light of the advances made by modern astronomy
and cosmology, and partly in response to the challenge of
philosophical pantheism (and to other factors such as the
feminist critique of patriarchal images of God) many Christian theologians in recent years have begun to revise the
classical image of a God who exists in sublime equanimity,
apart from the world, as a king sits serenely upon his throne.
Ideas of panentheism (God-in-the-world) have been explored
as a way of preserving both the immanence and transcendence of God. In this way of thinking, God is in the world and
the world is in God, but neither one is reducible to the other
(see, for example, McFague, 1987, pp. 59–78).

The notion of God as inhering in the world, yet as not
reducible to the world, has the attraction of aiming to retain
the main principle of classical theism, namely a God who is
transcendent to the world; yet it has the merit of overcoming
the dualism of God and world that an emphasis on God's
transcendence can generate. While this is often conceived to
be a particularly modern idea, encouraged by scientific discoveries, it is not at all new. It can be found, for example, in
Nicholas of Cusa's *De docta ignorantia* (*On Learned Ignorance,* 1440) where he encourages us to think of God as the
soul of the world, 'but without God's immersion in it' (Book 2,
Chapter 12). Whether panentheism as an attempt to rescue
the traditional Christian view of God as both immanent and
transcendent can hold these factors together is debatable. On
the one hand it is always susceptible to the collapse of transcendence into immanence, and thus prone to ending in
pantheism; and, on the other hand, it can seem as simply a
belated attempt to save the transcendent God of theism when
God can no longer be thought of as somehow 'outside' the
physical universe.

The wonderful discoveries of contemporary physics and cosmology offer us no religious certainty; there is no unequivocal and incontrovertible way to argue from the world back to a divine origination or ground of the world, namely God. Not only is it the case that the scientific evidence is ambiguous (we cannot provide conclusive evidence either for or against the existence of God) but more importantly, we realize that this approach is not going to produce God out of conceptual cosmic dust, as if God were capable of being discovered by means of an analysis of the data from the most recent cosmological discoveries. Or, to put this in traditional philosophical terms, it is not as if God could be grasped conceptually, by means of an act of understanding aided by evidence from the physical sciences, as a Being which exists distinct from beings as we know them. Further, it is perfectly plausible to understand the universe in a naturalistic way; a theistic explanation may be a simple and attractive one, but it cannot be deduced from the evidence and is most certainly not required.

In this regard philosopher John Searle expresses (an unintended) theological truth when he writes:

> For us, if it should turn out that God exists, that would have to be a fact of nature like any other. To the four basic forces in the universe – gravity, electromagnetism, weak and strong nuclear forces – we would add a fifth, the divine force. Or more likely, we would see the other forces as part of the divine force. But it would still be all physics, albeit divine physics. If the supernatural existed, it too would have to be natural. (Searle, 1999, p. 35)

Searle here is thinking about God understood as a Being, about whose existence we can argue, as we could argue about other mythological beings such as the griffin or the yeti. In so doing he is reflecting the way in which classical theism has traditionally thought of God, and he is correct to say that if we could discover such a God, then God would have to be part of nature. For how could such a Being 'exist' apart from the natural world, which is the only world we know? If we were to agree that this being 'existed', what other way would we have to think of her/him/it other than in the categories which applied to nature? Searle is right: God thought of in this way could only be another force of nature. It is, I think, this fundamental insight which, before the discoveries of modern cosmology, was behind the idea of pantheism: how can God, thought of as a Being, possibly be related to the natural world, which is the only world we know?

Thinking of God as a Being (infinitely greater in nature than the beings we encounter in this world) has contributed to a position where 'belief' and 'unbelief' are expected to hinge on the evidence. In our scientific age objective verification is the primary agreed standard of rationality. So scientists, theologians, philosophers and any reasonably informed person can enter the debate about whether or not the universe requires an originating cause, about whether the probability of this universe existing points to design or to chance. When this is done without an adequate reflection on the nature of the God who is the object of the evidence, then we reach a situation in which both sides of the argument are operating with a concept of God which is at the least problematic and at the worst unbelievable.

It is one of the ironies of the contemporary debates over science and religion that the classical theological tradition of understanding God as a metaphysical postulate of thought (the God of the so-called 'onto-theological' tradition) has been re-introduced by both defenders and opponents of the deity's existence. Some of the better theological commentators are aware of this: Ian Barbour comments, for example, that his own theological engagement with science should be seen not as part of a new natural theology (which would attempt to demonstrate the existence of God) but as framed within a 'theology of nature' which has its own foundations in 'a religious tradition based on religious experience and historical revelation' (Barbour, 2000, p. 31). This is true as far as it goes, but it does not lead to any resolution, because, as we have seen, appealing to contingent history to ground one's religious truth is an uncertain enterprise (see Chapter 6).

However, most theologians and scientists are products of a long Western philosophical and cultural tradition in which thought of God seems to default – as Searle does – to the classical onto-theological tradition of a Being which exists independently of the world, is its cause and can operate on it at will (whether that action is achieved through Newtonian or quantum mechanics is a secondary issue). When God is thought of in this way then the debates over the scientific evidence for design or the nature of the cause of the universe existing will remain unconsciously within a philosophical/theological tradition bound up with the logic of thinking in terms of the ontological difference between beings and Being. To put this theologically, it is to be constrained within the limits of always thinking of God as other than and separate from the world of which we are a part.

The physicist, philosopher and theologian, Willem Drees, advocates an understanding of God and of religion which accepts the truth of a naturalistic view of the world. He argues that 'a view of God which emphasises the unique, non-temporal character of God's existence and activity can be combined with a naturalist view of the natural world' (Drees, 1996, p. 272). Drees acknowledges that there are no obvious grounds for adopting this view of God and that it has limited *religious* significance in terms of the devotional practices in which believers commonly engage; in this view of God, concrete religious traditions seem to be bypassed. Having argued, as I have here, that there is no basis in physics (or, indeed, biology) for drawing positive conclusions about the existence of God, Drees also excludes particular historical traditions as bases for such belief. We have no grounds to assume that there is 'a basis in the historical realm where none was found in the physical and biological realms' (p. 273). As I have argued in Chapter 6, the contingencies of history do not offer us religious truth; theological approaches to God through historical revelation seek 'gaps' in the natural world, this time in historical and psychological processes rather than in the natural processes discovered by physics and biology.

In Drees' pared-down theology we can only have a Kantian minimum of belief, namely 'belief in the philosophical proposition that there is a transcendent entity to which the natural world owes its existence' (p. 274). But this leaves us with a concept of God detached from the richness of the world religions. How are we to bring these two strands together, if at all? Drees suggests that we view the world's religions from an evolutionary perspective, where human beings (like other organisms) are studied in relation to their environments, including in our case our religious environment. Drees is surely correct when he asserts that there is no reason to dismiss religious traditions out of hand as being in perpetual conflict with natural science; they are, after all, complex human cultures which serve to orient our lives within the biological and cultural contexts in which we live (p. 277). But they should not over-reach their boundaries of competence: 'religions should not propose answers which are at odds with what is known, nor should they wish to propose answers which upset the integrity of the world as discerned through the natural sciences' (p. 281).

Drees' final suggestion is very much along the lines of what I myself consider to be the best way to understand the relationship between our religious traditions and the possibility of a God. 'God' can be thought of as a 'regulative ideal', a possibility thrown up by the very nature of reality as we experience it; this does not at all preclude the existence of a transcendent being, but it does not require it. As a regulative ideal, 'God' offers us a transcendent horizon by which some of us might choose to judge reality as experienced in our here-and-now historical existence. Our religions, with their very particular traditions of symbols, doctrines, worship and ethical systems, give us very particular possibilities for responding to our historical context in the light of this transcendent horizon, but they too must always come under critique. This will result in a certain relativizing of all religious beliefs, and even a breaking down of the barriers surrounding what we consider to be 'religious'. As Drees puts it: 'That religions embody a sense of transcendence with respect to our situation is not a peculiar consequence of phenomena which already have the label "religion"; rather, it is the kind of characteristic which makes us label certain phenomena religious' (p. 282). Religion is that which helps (some of) us respond to the world as we encounter it and does so in the light of a transcendent horizon of possibility, a horizon that we can call 'God'.

In the final analysis, the physical universe offers us no incontestable answers; whether we opt for theism or deism, pantheism or panentheism, agnosticism or atheism, will depend to a great extent on the personal experiences, hopes, desires, loves and fears which we have as individual human beings living in this world. Perhaps the biggest mistake made in this whole current debate is the idea that the existence of God is an issue that can be somehow determined either way, even in terms of probability; it is not, for the question of God is something that is answered in the hearts of individual people and not by publicly available evidence. It is little surprise, then, that arguments between the more traditional believing theologians and anti-religious atheistic scientists, about whether or not the universe points to the existence of God, seem to be like new wine poured into old wine-skins.

8

Beyond the Idol

We should stop thinking about God as someone, over there, way up there, transcendent, and, what is more – into the bargain, precisely – capable, more than any satellite orbiting in space, of seeing into the most secret of the interior places. It is perhaps necessary, if we are to follow the traditional Judeo-Christian–Islamic injunction, but also at the risk of turning it against that tradition, to think of God and the name of God without such idolatrous stereotyping or representation. Then we might say: God is the name of the possibility I have of keeping a secret that is visible from the interior but not from the exterior. (Jacques Derrida, *The Gift of Death*, 1995)

One surprising aspect of the cultural and intellectual trend which, for want of a better term, we can call 'postmodernity' is that there has been a renewal of interest in the question of God. Perhaps more accurately, there has been a renewal of interest in the possibilities opened up by the postmodern critique of the modern critique of religion. There is space again for the question of God among the varied discourses of postmodernity, and this space could tentatively be termed 'sacred', not merely because of its uncanny and unexpected emergence, but also with respect to the possibilities which it allows for us to think creatively again about the question of

God. The great metanarratives of modernity, among which we can number progress, Marxism, Freudianism, the bureaucratic state, and the autonomous individual, were themselves developed partly out of a critique of religion and a rejection of God (invariably understood as the interfering parent from whom we must move away in order to be truly free).

But the postmodern turn enabled the insight that modernity's metanarratives themselves rested on shaky foundations and were incapable of offering any ultimate justification of their own stories. Thus, it might be equally viable to speak of modernity's second critique as to speak of 'postmodernity' as such; if modernity's first critique was its attack on the naïvety and obscurantism which it saw as characteristic of the medieval world, then modernity's second critique is its insight into its own limitations. In a third 'Copernican revolution' postmodernity turns its gaze towards the space within which we might just glimpse the impossible, the moment in which the realization occurs that hope might be fulfilled. If the premodern worldview focused on God in a realist sense, and if the modern focused on the human subject as a replacement for the divine, then the postmodern worldview focuses on the space wherein both God and self – no longer understood as entities capable of being confined by concepts – might be encountered anew. This cultural space, or clearing, offers a renewed possibility for us here and now, at this time and in this cultural context. It is a possibility which presents an opportunity for hope; not hope for some future state of being, but hope for an encounter in and of the present.

But 'hope is not hope if its object is seen' (Romans 8.24). Our postmodern condition is inevitably one of uncertainty and deferral, and while many of us may hope for safe havens in politics, morals, religion or art, we must now live with the realization that we can never expect that hope to be fulfilled. If God is the ultimate symbol of our hope, then postmodernity's awareness of the fragility of all cultural and religious symbols and ideas forces us back to the realization that all certainty eludes us. It is this realization of the inevitability of infinite deferral – feared and repressed – which at least partly accounts for the vehemence of the many reactive forces evident in our world today, especially among many of the world's great religions. We see in our current religious situation many reactionary attempts to avoid the inevitable truth that there is no final answer; yet in the postmodern journey the definitive encounter with the divine always eludes us, for it is always beyond. God as God can never be grasped by our reasoning, for if 'reason's last step is the recognition that there are an infinite number of things which are beyond it' (Pascal, 1966 [1670], p. 85) then our faltering steps towards the divine are always taken in the knowledge that we have only just learned to walk and that the journey is endless.

If we encounter the divine we cannot expect to be addressed directly like Moses was, but we might occasionally just imagine the faint remnant of a former presence, like the lingering odour of a once burning bush; we know that something happened here even if we cannot tell what it was. So, perhaps when we enter sacred space we will not recognize it, for the trail is not marked ahead of us and there are no pointers to tell us where we have arrived. Our final destination is always on the horizon and it is the journey which is its own fulfilment. Perhaps we realize that the promised land was always an unattainable dream and we wander, not this time in the desert but in a forest of meanings, surrounded, disoriented, living with the displacement that is simultaneously our hope and our despair. On this journey we have no map and the most we can hope is that we are found.

In our postmodern wanderings we now find ourselves in a new situation, one in which the religious – including, inevitably, the question of God – emerges with renewed vigour; the repressed returns, albeit now in different, even contradictory, guises. In this situation we cannot encounter 'God' in a naïve premodern sense – other than in the many 'fundamentalisms' which see in the critique of the modern a new opportunity for reaction – but rather in the unexpected, the uncanny, even the unbelievable. In this situation we cannot have the confidence of our great predecessors and think that God is within our grasp (even if we don't always realize it). Augustine of Hippo thought it remarkable how God could dwell in some souls who do not know him, yet not dwell in some souls who do know him. He concluded that: '[O]ne group could know God but not possess Him; the other could possess Him before they know Him. But happiest are those to whom knowing God is the same as possessing Him, for that is the most adequate, true and happy knowledge' (Augustine, *On the Presence of God*, 1984, p. 414). Similarly, Pascal (drawing, I think, on Augustine) thought that it was possible to divide humanity neatly into three religious groups: 'There are only three sorts of people: those who have found God and serve him; those who are busy seeking him and have not found him; those who live without either seeking or finding him. The first are reasonable and happy, the last are foolish and unhappy, those in the middle are unhappy and reasonable' (Pascal, 1966 [1670], p. 82). But our situation is unlike either that of premodernity or the dawn of modernity, for it is when we think that we have found God it is most likely that we have not. We neither 'know' nor 'possess' the sacred and the most we can hope for is that we persevere in our wandering. On our postmodern journey, 'the most adequate, true and happy knowledge' is always just out of reach.

If our hope for the sacred is worth holding on to, then it can only be hope in the form of a longing for the unattainable, for in so longing we do not so much aspire to reach the object of our hope but rather we hope that our hope does not fail. Our longing in this respect is the reason for 'hope beyond hope'. To hope in a context of pluralism, where there are many and varied possibilities for meaning and yet only one true option for meaninglessness (the rejection of all values), we can no longer hope like Augustine and Pascal for an eschatological fulfilment in a world beyond this one: eternal life, the immortal soul, the heavenly communion of the saints, the beatific vision itself. When we are told that death is the end, when the soul is extinguished with the firing of the brain's last synapse, for what then can we hope? We can only hope that our hope may continue, that we do not fall into despair. Our longing is that our hope and our actions may be worthwhile, but as for its object as understood by traditional religion, it is no longer within our gaze. Our hope is only the longing for the impossible, the limit of our desire for a presence that is always absent.

This postmodern longing for the impossible, a longing which keeps hope alive, is of course only one perspective in a field of many potentialities. There are always others who see it differently, and who feel that our salvation is within reach. In the present age (whatever name we may give it) we have witnessed the return of God in the guise of the reassertion of the religious in strong ethnic, political, tribal and nationalist movements. This return may be unwelcome to many but it should be a surprise only to those for whom religion marks merely a passing stage, an era (albeit a long one) in the coming-of-age of humanity into the bright future of rational control of ourselves, our world and our destiny. Yet powerful forces often give rise to their opposites, and the eventual disappearance of religion has for some time been the accepted wisdom of the Western intelligentsia. But from the other side of the postmodern coin, what better legitimation is there for one's political views than that they have divine authorization?

Yet in this manipulation and utilization of the divine, however sincerely held, we do not encounter the uncanny, the unforeseen, the unexpected. We encounter primarily the face of the zealot, the one who would will the divine into action on his behalf, the one who would provoke the apocalypse not in his own name but in that of God. Perhaps the space opened up by modernity's new lack of confidence in its own project of rationalization opens also the space for its opposite, that which has been repressed, the return to the religious intolerance it had considered vanquished. Whatever the reasons for this return of the religious in political forms, we are witnessing the reappearance of the divine, in a mode until recently thought to be unlikely: to cite only some of the most obvious examples, we see this re-emergence of the divine in the foundation of social order through religious law (Islam in Iran, Sudan, Nigeria), in nationalist/religious identity (Hinduism in India), in right-wing politics (in the Bible belt of the southern USA).

In these 'returns' the divine functions to bind again that which would otherwise be in danger of disintegration; it is used to force back together the fragments of society and the religious order of the community and the self. In these old–new manifestations, 'God' functions again in a way that Nietzsche thought was disappearing for ever from the consciousness of the West. Perhaps this return of God was inevitable, for there is no greater force to have on one's side than the might of the divine itself. If there is anything surprising about this situation it is that it has happened so soon; God has come back before God was fully gone away. But this return of the divine in the guise of politico-tribal identities is inevitably characterized by the indelible mark of violence, either real or symbolic: real violence in physical destruction of life, property and whole communities, and symbolic violence in laws, symbols, rituals and cultural practices, which enforce exclusion, oppression and victimization. And it cannot be otherwise, for this God of the tribe can only be the God of vengeance, always the God of triumph, of possession and of segregation.

If we are to perceive, however faintly, the uncanny return of God we will not encounter it directly in the guise of religious, tribal and political violence. However, strangely, by alerting us to the sterility of all such violence, these reactionary movements may well be the stimulus that leads us to other possibilities. Perhaps, in such a polarized world, our task is first of all to listen more keenly and receive that which comes first to us. The Italian philosopher Gianni Vattimo, in his short book *Credere di Credere* explores just such a possibility (the title is better translated as *To Believe in Belief*, rather than the slightly misleading title of the English translation, *Belief* (1999)). Vattimo reflects on his own return to a form of 'belief' by means of a changed understanding of God occasioned by a weakening of the philosophical notion of 'Being' in some recent Western philosophy. Specifically, Vattimo brings together the critique of the history of metaphysics undertaken by Nietzsche and Heidegger, and the reinterpretation of the Christian understanding of Jesus' sacrificial death by René Girard, to explore what constitutes 'belief' when secularization is itself interpreted in religious terms. Through his reading of these two, distinct, trajectories of modern/postmodern thought, Vattimo can now say that he believes that he believes.

From Girard, Vattimo takes the idea that the violent death of Jesus, far from being the epitome of the sacrificial appeasement of a vengeful God, is rather the unmasking of all violence as sacred in origin. According to Girard's far-reaching theory, religious ritual has its origins in the repetition of an originating act of violence. This violence is stimulated through the human capacity to imitate, most importantly to recognize and to imitate the desire of another. This is what Girard calls 'mimetic desire', desire as imitation of the desire of the other, in which the object of desire is what is desired by the other (we see this effect most clearly in children who not only want what the other child has, but also want what the other child wants; it is equally present in our adult behaviour, but we perceive it less readily).

This imitative desire is a self-reinforcing process, until eventually violence ensues over that which is desired. Peace between individuals or in the community is then restored by means of the victimization of one individual (or select group), a process which we see too often on our news programmes. Paradoxically, due to the effect of what Girard calls the 'scapegoat mechanism' the victim becomes the saviour of the community:

> By a scapegoat effect I mean that strange process through which two or more people are reconciled at the expense of a third party who appears guilty or responsible for whatever ails, disturbs or frightens the scapegoaters. They feel relieved of their tension and they coalesce into a more harmonious group. They now have a single purpose, which is to prevent the scapegoat from harming them, by expelling and destroying him. (Girard, 1996, p. 12)

With the scapegoating comes a renewed sense of purpose and a feeling of lost unity restored; and this achievement is celebrated by the ritual re-enactment of the sacrificial act. In a seeming paradox, the victim is a sacred entity because it is through the victim that social cohesion is achieved.

Girard's insight into the effect of the scapegoat mechanism brings to the forefront the role of the victim in dissipating the violence which inheres in social rivalry resulting from imitative desire. Crucially, for the scapegoat effect to work it is essential that the victim is perceived as truly responsible for the community's difficulties; once this is understood we can comprehend the astonishing fact that most violent mobs really do believe in the guilt of their victim/s, even those whom outsiders perceive as totally without blame. To allow for one moment the innocence of the victim to intrude on the group's conscious objective would be to undermine the eventual unity which the violence achieves.

Now, Girard contends, the Christian New Testament undoes this mechanism by recognizing that Jesus is the victim who is innocent. If the victim mechanism results in social cohesion through violence (that act which binds society together by means of the sacrifice of a scapegoat victim who then becomes sacralized) then the true revelation of the New Testament is that violence is the basis of culture. Against a long theological tradition, Girard asserts that the 'Christ of the Gospels dies against sacrifice, and through his death, he reveals its nature and origin by making sacrifice unworkable ... and bringing sacrificial culture to an end' (Girard, 1996, p. 18). If Jesus is the victim who is recognized as innocent, then any actual culture which perceives this revelation is itself unmasked and undone, for it cannot live with the knowledge that the victim is always arbitrary and that social cohesion (including art, religion, custom, law and all that *binds*) is founded on the blood of the innocent. But this is too much truth to bear, for the fear of the unleashing of uncontrolled violence is still too great, and so even Christian theology (perhaps, ironically and tragically, *especially* Christian theology) continues to perpetuate sacralized violence through its perception of Jesus as the perfect victim, fulfilling the salvific plan of the deity.

Vattimo interprets this unveiling of sacred violence at the foundation of culture as the undoing of the God of natural theology and of metaphysics. He thinks that it finally exposes the God of philosophy, whose attributes of omnipotence, omniscience, omnipresence, eternity and transcendence are the characteristics of power and dominance. In Vattimo's view, Girard's insights finally uncover the violence underlying the metaphysical concept of God, which has come under attack in the deconstruction of metaphysics pursued by Nietzsche, Heidegger, Derrida and others. The violent God of primal sacrifice, the God who demands appeasement for the sin of Adam and Eve, and the all-powerful *ipsum esse subsistens* of the metaphysical tradition are one and the same.

Vattimo's reading of these parallel and complementary lines of critique leads him to conclude that the secularizing impulse of modernity is itself partly an effect of the Christian gospel's destabilizing effect on the culture of the violent sacred. Viewed from the unsettling perspective of the revelation of Jesus as the unveiling of the complicity of violence with the sacred, it is possible that the loss of religious mystique in the modern world (what Max Weber called the demystifying – *entzauberung* – of modernity) 'is precisely a positive effect of Jesus' teaching, and not a way of moving away from it' (Vattimo, 1999, p. 41). Of course, the effect of the demystifying impulse of modernity is not confined to the narrow sphere of the 'religious' as a discrete and isolated component of culture, but extends to all those cultural, social and political entities which explicitly or implicitly claim their authority through sacral association: quasi-sacred entities such as the 'State', 'Monarchy, the 'Nation', the 'Father', 'Democracy', 'Truth', 'Memory', 'History', and the 'Self' have their violent foundations unveiled.

If this is an accurate telling of the origin of human culture, then the unmasking of the sacral quality of violence should shake the foundations of our cultural and social icons. The Christian gospel, with its message of the innocence of the victim, far from bringing peace, might well be bringing conflict, but this time it is a conflict *which cannot be resolved through further violence*, for the innocence of Jesus reveals the innocence of all victims. The sacred, too, is demystified as its complicity in violence is unveiled, and the innocence of the victim continues to insinuate itself into the consciousness of the culture. If Girard is correct, there is no escaping the continued debt of the culture of the West to the Jewish and

Christian traditions, even if in this respect that debt remains largely unknown or, perhaps, known but unacknowledged.

The import of these insights for a reading of traditional incarnational theology is profound. What New Testament Christology calls the *kenosis* (emptying) involved in the descent of God to humanity in the person of Jesus (Philippians 2.7) can now be read as both the confirmation of the innocence of all victims through the full identification of the divine with the victim, and at the same time the final rejection of all attempts to reveal the divine as power, as dominance, as true knowledge, as infinity or as law. These latter attributes reveal the mark of a metaphysics of violence by attributing to the deity the highest aspirations of a culture of power, and must be rejected in the name of God and in the name of the innocent victim (which orthodox Christianity perceived to be one and the same).

However, we cannot resolve here the complex question of whether Girard's theory lends more credibility to orthodox Christian doctrine (he thinks that it does) or whether it remains simply a fascinating insight into the anthropology of religion. However, I would suggest that this identification of the divine with the innocent victim marks the end of any naïve reading of revelation as divine intervention in history, which I have criticized earlier. If anything, Girard's theory supports a critique of theologies of divine intervention and the corresponding idea of revelation as information from beyond this world. From the perspective of the victim, ideas of God's exclusive dealings with one group to the exclusion of all others can be seen to be another manifestation of the scapegoat mechanism, and can only be sustained by anthropomorphic concepts of God marked by violence.

So Girard's theory must remain above all an anthropological insight, not a basis for theological knowledge of God or, in the more nuanced style of contemporary theology, a revelation of God's very 'self'. In a word, as we saw in the case of Job, the anthropomorphic, or even andropomorphic, God is unmasked. For this God can only be the perpetrator of sacred violence, a less than pale imitation of our very selves. What we can learn from Girard, however, is that under the cultural influence of the Christian gospel itself we should no longer be willing to pay the cost of religious unity and compliance.

Vattimo perceives here also a connection between this history of metaphysics marked by violence and the historical authoritarianism of the Christian Church. The history of religious authoritarianism in Christianity is closely bound up with the history of metaphysics, 'the idea that there is an objective truth of Being which once recognized (by reason, enlightened by faith), becomes the stable basis of dogmatic theology and above all of moral teaching, which claims to be grounded upon the eternal nature of things' (Vattimo, 1999, p. 49). The symbolic and, sadly, the real violence unleashed by the Church throughout its history is bound up both with the image of the sacred violence which attempts to ensure the stability and coherence of the community and with the history of metaphysics under the rubric of dogmatic theology (it is not incidental, I think, that Pope John Paul II prefers to speak of the Roman Catholic Church as a *sacred* society).

The real *kenosis* revealed by the theology of the incarnation cannot be comprehended within the history of metaphysics because there the temptation to docetism – to belief in the mere *appearance* of the emptying of the divine fullness – is always too powerful. From this perspective we can see with fresh eyes the impulse towards the critique of the metaphysical God inherent in Christian theology's insistence on the real humanity of the Christ. The self-limitation of God in the Christian idea of incarnation, the *kenosis* which marks divine outpouring into the human, is carried on in the weakening of Being which is revealed at the 'end' of metaphysics. Viewed from this perspective, secularization can be read as the continuation of *kenosis*. The divine is revealed as weakening, as self-abandonment, and as de-sacralization. So when the complicity of the sacred with violence and with what Vattimo calls 'a metaphysical–naturalistic conception of God' is thus understood, we can only view secularization as itself part of the impact of Christianity on Western culture, an element in the separation of the gospel from the violent structures of natural religion underpinned and legitimated by an ontology of objective truth.

In what manner, then, can we speak again of faith or of belief in this context? If a secular philosopher has re-discovered the truth of the Christian gospel in Girard's unmasking of sacred violence, and has perceived also an ineluctable link to the symbolic violence of the history of metaphysics, what can it mean to return to 'belief' from this vantage point? Vattimo is adamant that for him it cannot be a return to a body of doctrines and precepts, clearly defined and accepted as a discipline. Nor for him, as someone whose context is in the Catholic Church, can it be a return to the moral discipline of that Church, characterized as it is by what he regards as a superstitious fundamentalism which marks much of its ethical teaching.

Vattimo is also critical of what he regards as the 'tragic' concept of Christianity – the idea that the world is, so to speak, falling apart under the twin onslaught of the philosophical critique of knowledge and the will-to-power inhering in our techno-scientific culture, and that the only option is to turn towards the 'wholly other' who is revealed as the transcendent God, our last hope when the world of human beings has failed us. But this 'tragic and apocalyptic Christianity . . . is merely the equally unacceptable inversion of the Christianity that believed that it could legitimize itself via traditional metaphysics' (1999, p. 83). Vattimo thinks that in its institutional religious form this tragic view of the world tends towards a regressive fundamentalism and in its secular, philosophical, form (as in Levinas and Derrida) it tends to have a levelling and reductive effect *vis-à-vis* the historicity of existence, for it reduces the particularity of existence to a 'vertical' relation to the Other.

Whether Vattimo is correct or not in this latter claim – and it is at least disputable – his main contention is that the renewal of interest in religion shown by some contemporary philosophy should not be tempted towards a tragic Christian view of the world, for such a view has not recognized the *kenosis* at the heart of the Christian gospel and 'thus falls back on a conception of God which not only presents all the traits of the metaphysical God . . . but also explicitly retrieves the personal authority characteristic of the pre-metaphysical God of the natural religions' (Vattimo, 1999, p. 84). As I have argued in the case of Job, there is nothing to be gained from calling on God the Just One to rescue you from God the Wrathful One, for this serves only to return us to the (literally) vicious circle of power, punishment and retribution.

So, if we can no longer think of God in metaphysical terms (as the all-powerful Being) and if God as God has been conceived by the philosophical tradition of the West in terms of an ontological/metaphysical tradition of Being which itself has been relentlessly critiqued, then how can we think of God at all in our present situation? As Vattimo suggests, it can only ever be a form of weak and tenuous belief, in which we believe that we believe. It can only be a searching after, never a knowing, or a holding on to. It can only be, perhaps, what Derrida suggests in the passage which opens this chapter: the name of a possibility.

French philosopher Jean-Luc Marion, in his influential book *God Without Being* (1991), asks us to attempt to think of God without thinking of God in terms of the philosophical concept, 'Being'. The God who was characterized by the ontological distinction between Being and beings ends up as an idol through its objectification in the conceptual categories of a philosophical system: 'When a philosophical thought expresses a concept of what it then names "God", this concept functions exactly as an idol' (p. 16).

This idea of God as a 'Being' is the creation of the philosophical gaze, a result of the drive to objectification which is the hallmark of the history of metaphysics. It is the God which is argued about by 'theism' and 'atheism' and it is the God which can only be a projection of the human. Marion challenges us to think of God as that which cannot be conceptualized, as that which can never be brought into a philosophical or linguistic category or grasped as an idea: 'Concerning God, let us admit that we can think him only under the figure of the unthinkable, but of an unthinkable that exceeds as much what we cannot think as what we can; for that which I may not think is still the concern of *my* thought, and hence to *me* remains thinkable' (p. 46).

God, in this view, is beyond theism and beyond atheism. Here we have a possibility to overcome the limitations of the God about whom we can argue as we argue over objects or concepts, about whom we could somehow reach a conclusion, about whom we could say that we have settled the matter once and for all. To think God as unthinkable is to reject the idolatry of the God of onto-theology, the God over whom theists and atheists argue and it is to admit that we can no longer 'blaspheme the unthinkable in an idol' (p. 46), an idol created out of the concepts within which the metaphysical tradition of Western philosophy and theology had demarcated God. Marion thinks that our traditional concept of 'God' is permanently marked with the stigma of the conceit that we can think 'God' or grasp 'God' in a concept, and he invites us to henceforth write the word G̶o̶d̶ under the sign of an erasure to indicate that we are not describing, grasping, conceptualizing or controlling the divine; yet we remain in a state in which God's very 'unthinkableness saturates our thought – right from the beginning and for ever' (p. 47). If Marion is correct, if God cannot be captured in a concept, then the new

guardians of the golden calf are revealed to be those systematic theologians who set out to grasp the divine in an ontology
of doctrine. As I have argued, doctrines and dogmas – even
those like 'Trinity' – are a groping in the darkness of the
history of metaphysics, not the bright light of divine truth
shining through our ignorance.

But now, if we are to attempt to think the unthinkable,
'what name, what concept, and what sign nevertheless yet
remain feasible?' What can we say at all about God/G⊠d?
Marion argues that a single concept remains, that of love, for
God is love (1 John 4.8), and we experience that love as pure
gift. In the giving of God we come to know what love is: 'what
is peculiar to love consists in the fact that it gives itself . . .
[and in knowing God in this way we can perceive that] no condition can continue to restrict his initiative, amplitude and
ecstasy. Love loves without condition, simply because it loves;
he thus loves without limit or restriction' (Marion, 1991, p.
47). In Marion's view we can continue to think of God/G⊠d as
love only by seeing that love as a continuing giving, an excess
of abandonment 'without end or limit', and we can never fix
this love as an idol because it is always beyond us in an
unceasing gesture of the gift that subverts the impulse to
create the idol through an outpouring which holds nothing
back.

For Marion, 'God can give himself to be thought without
idolatry only starting from himself alone: to give himself to be
thought as love, hence as gift; to give himself to be thought as
a thought of the gift. Or better, as a gift for thought, as a gift
that gives itself to be thought' (p. 49). Thus, by being removed
to the untouchable realm of the unthinkable which gives
itself as gift, is God saved from the clutches of metaphysics
and returned to God-as-God, always beyond our understanding; in this respect Marion stands within the tradition of
negative theology which we have already encountered.

Yet, is there not something unreal about Marion's all-too-easy identification of God and love? In attempting to escape metaphysics, does he not return to anthropomorphism? And, is it not the case that the wrath of God as well as the love of God is also part of the character of the anthropomorphic God, for how can we accept one aspect of God's character without encountering the other? As most of the Christian tradition – particularly popular piety, but also theologians from Augustine to Calvin and beyond – saw very clearly, if you want God as traditionally understood then you cannot have love without anger, forgiveness without vengeance, mercy without justice, heaven without hell. Throughout Christian history there have been those who sought the love of God without the wrath, and in Marion we have another such optimist. Yes, fortunate indeed are those few who can experience the ceaseless gift-giving of this postmodern, post-metaphysical God.

Professional philosophers and theologians may have the luxury of resorting to a refined concept of God; but the return of God in postmodernity is not only to be found in the speculations of philosophers but in the many popular politico–religious movements which now come under the umbrella term of 'fundamentalism' (not an ideal term, although a useful one). Is it not the strangest of the many strange aspects of the postmodern that God returns in such different, even contradictory guises: here in the postmodern critique of metaphysics, there in the prayer of the suicide bomber? One of the many ways in which we can read the explosion of fundamentalist thinking in our postmodern age is as an element *within* the postmodern, not as a reaction against it. Rejecting yet simultaneously taking advantage of the pluralism of our age, fundamentalists have seized the postmodern day, and have realized that if the vain attempt of secular modernity to found a just and lasting peace on rational principles failed in the horrors of the gulags, of Hiroshima and of Treblinka, then something else was called for, something which did not require the rational and universal foundations which the secular spirit thought it could provide.

As postmodernism brought its ironic critique to bear on the fragile certainties of the modernist vision of progress – and in this is it not merely the belated and self-conscious high-cultural counterpart to the failure of 'progress' in the death camps, the famines, the biological weapons and child labour? – others saw the edifice crumbling and decided to rebuild on what they thought was more solid, older ground. 'Fundamentalism' in its many forms is an expression of the postmodern critique of the modern; it is simply the other possibility, the alternative choice that is available to us when a culture's appetite and aptitude for public critique have been attenuated to the degree that has occurred in the contemporary West.

With postmodernity's weakening of modernity's critical spirit came the freedom for everyone, not just the postmodern intellectual-as-ironist, to decline to justify their beliefs in a publicly accountable way. If everyone is entitled to their beliefs no matter what they are, and any cultural coherence which is left to us is disintegrating before our eyes, then why not place oneself squarely within a secure and self-contained belief-system, a system which itself is placed beyond question? For those who choose this path, it is the belonging which matters and thus we can see that the content of one's beliefs, although they are of importance to their adherents, matter less than the fact that they are held, and held with conviction; it is the believing that permits the centre to hold, not the believed-in. For the postmodern fundamentalist, *J'y suis et j'y reste.*

In the end, modernity's attempt to keep together the secular spirit of rational accountability and the myth of progress was an impossible and unsustainable dream. As the myth of progress collapsed it took down with it modernity's assumption of a shared rationality and aspiration for social, cultural, psychological and aesthetic coherence; after the death of God, as Nietzsche knew, comes the death of much else that we hold sacred. Into the space vacated by the collapse of the myth of progress and rationality came, on the one side, the new soldier of God and, on the other side, the postmodern perspectivist or ironist. In their extreme forms, the former tendency turns quickly to violence as the most effective method of achieving a goal which requires no justification other than that of being believed, and the latter tendency lauds its inability to distinguish any value from any other value or non-value on the spurious and ultimately incoherent grounds that no one can judge anyone else's cultural practice (because we can only see the world from our own bounded perspective, which is no better or worse than any other). These two diametrically opposed, and equally fallacious, faces of our contemporary political and cultural situation constitute the twin polarities of the collapse of modernity's highest ideals. Unfortunately, in the return of God under the rubric of fundamentalism, reactionary religion enters the space where irony fears to tread.

In a cultural situation in which we have worldviews as antithetic as the postmodernist culture of irony and the emergence of various fundamentalisms, mutual misunderstanding is the order of the day (as the case of the *fatwah* against Salman Rushdie so clearly illustrates); the ironist looks with bewilderment on the religious zealotry which he had thought was gone for good, and the fundamentalist views the secular culture of postmodernity as merely the epitome of all that is tearing the world apart. Yet in this context of mutual mistrust, even loathing, there is something that the fundamentalist (but, thankfully, not the fundamentalist alone) sees that the perspectivist does not (or chooses not to). This is summed up well by Andrew Delbanco: 'Without reverence for *something* there can be no proscriptions – and it should be clear enough to any observer of contemporary culture that we are short on both' (1995, p. 211).

In the end, God is not and cannot ever be a panacea for our contemporary political and cultural ills. God thus understood is little more than the product of misguided theological uses of history and metaphysics: a God who can be nothing more than our own image. Still, the question of God is never closed, as many atheists and theists think. To seek such a closure, in either direction, is to mistake an epistemological possibility for a cognitive certainty, and to replace an existential possibility with a metaphysical idol. It is precisely its openness which makes the question of God so intriguing and so inescapable.

In the end, as the history of negative theology so aptly demonstrates, the greatest wisdom in relation to God is to remain silent. We have to learn, therefore, how *not* to talk about God (unfortunately, to learn this we have to say something). This learning how not to talk is perhaps a skill we might cultivate along the lines suggested by one of our greatest contemporary thinkers in this area, Raimon Panikkar. God, suggests Panikkar, is 'an invocation', one who is called to or upon, not one who is affirmed or negated by our cognitive abilities. Through his knowledge of the religious cultures of East and West, Panikkar seeks to bring together the Western emphasis on 'the limit experience of Being and Plenitude . . . attracted by the world of things as they reveal to us the transcendence of Reality' with the Eastern concern with 'the consciousness-limit of Nothing and Emptiness . . . attracted by the world of the subject, which reveals to us the impermanence of that very Reality' (1997, p. 149).

To help us overcome the conflict between the possibilities of, on the one hand, a God who is nothing more than a caricature of ourselves and, on the other hand, belief in nothing at all, Panikkar suggests nine ways *not* to talk about God; these nine ways are formulated in positive terms but the converse is easily imagined. His suggestions are as follows (in paraphrase with my comments in parentheses).

1. An interior silence is necessary for anyone who wants to talk of God (leave your preconceived ideas behind).
2. Talking about God is not like talking about anything else (to objectify God in any thought or word is to talk about an idol).
3. It is our entire being which talks of God (there is no special rational or emotional perspective, no privileged discourse, to access God).
4. God does not belong to the churches, to religion, to science, or to any other human activity (warning: your theology might be at best arrogance, at worst sectarianism).
5. We still need religious language, symbols and beliefs (such expressions, including those of more traditional religion, are inescapable; but remember that when the wise woman points at the moon the foolish man sometimes looks at the finger).
6. God is a symbol, not a concept (there is no interpretive key to explain what 'God' might mean, so theologians can stop looking for it).
7. Just as there are many human cultures, there are many ways to talk about God (there is no 'correct' way of speaking of God, including this one, by which we could judge other ways of speaking about God).
8. What 'God' means can be expressed by other words or symbols, or even none, for God is not the possession of those who express belief (theists do not own God, and cultural pluralism alerts us to the contingency of all our language, including the most sacred).
9. All talk of God ends in a renewed silence (enough said, but let this not be an excuse for what Panikkar calls 'cowardice or frivolity').

Were we wise enough to take this sage advice, we might just hear something in the silence.

Conclusion

Ten Theses on God (but not the last word).

1. We can never know for certain whether God 'exists' or does 'not exist'. However, if God is not thought of in a naïve sense as an extra-worldly Being, then this question ceases to have meaning in the way in which it is usually expressed.
2. The question of God is not a matter of a dispute about evidence, which can be resolved by rational argument and evaluation of the balance of probabilities. It is rather a question concerning each person's response to the whole of their existence.
3. You can look at the cosmos and see the wonders of the Creator or you can look at the cosmos and see the astonishing self-regulating properties of matter. Religiously speaking, the universe is ambiguous.
4. Religious doctrines and beliefs are not information about an extra-worldly Being or insight into another world beyond or after this one; they are each a specific community's attempts to give voice to its experience of the sacred as encountered in history.
5. God is not a 'Being' which can be conceptualized in any philosophy or theology, any word or any thought. Each attempt to grasp God in this way, no matter how venerated or sophisticated, is idolatry, just another golden calf.

6. Each encounter with the most profound depth of our co-dependent selves, with each other, and with the natural world which produced us and on which we depend, is an encounter with 'God'. Transcendence and immanence are one.

7. Where 'God' is used by believers of any theistic religion as the legitimation of any form of violence – physical, mental or socio-cultural, then 'God' must be rejected in the name of humanity. The indictment of this 'God' is one of the lessons of the Book of Job.

8. 'God' is a symbol or metaphor for the totality of everything we consider to be of absolute value and meaning for us (but it is not the only such symbol). Concrete religious traditions, with their prayers, rituals, symbols, doctrines, are necessary human historical expressions of particular communities' encounter with this totality.

9. Pain and suffering are part of the nature of the universe we inhabit. We should abandon anthropomorphic ideas of God which expect outside intervention to alter the laws of nature in response to our pleading.

10. When we turn to God-as-God (and not as an idol), silence is the most profound response.

References and Bibliography

Aquinas, Thomas (1955) *Summa Contra Gentiles; Book One: God*, translated with introduction and notes by Anton C. Pegis. Notre Dame and London: University of Notre Dame Press.

Aquinas, Thomas (1989) *Summa Theologiae: A Concise Translation*, Timothy McDermott (ed.). Allen, Texas: Christian Classics.

Armstrong, Karen (1993) *A History of God*. New York: Ballantine Books.

Armstrong, Karen (2000) *The Battle for God*. New York: Alfred A. Knopf.

Arnold, Matthew (1994) *Dover Beach and Other Poems*. New York: Dover Publications.

Augustine of Hippo (1984), 'On the Presence of God', in *Selected Writings*, translated with introduction by Mary T. Clark. Mahwah, NJ: Paulist Press.

Ayer, A. J. and Jane O'Grady (eds) (1992) *A Dictionary of Philosophical Quotations*. Oxford: Blackwell.

Bailie, Gil (1997) *Violence Unveiled: Humanity at the Crossroads*. New York: Crossroad.

Barbour, Ian G. (1990) *Religion in an Age of Science*. London: SCM Press.

Barbour, Ian G. (2000) *When Science Meets Religion: Enemies, Strangers or Partners?* San Francisco: Harper/San Francisco.

Barnes, Timothy D. (1981) *Constantine and Eusebius*. Cambridge, MA: Harvard University Press.

Barnes, Timothy D. (1993) *Athanasius and Constantius: Theology and Politics in the Constantinian Empire*. Cambridge, MA: Harvard University Press.

Barrow, John and Frank Tipler (1986) *The Anthropic Cosmological Principle*. Oxford and New York: Oxford University Press.

Bauman, Zygmunt (1997) *Postmodernity and Its Discontents*. Cambridge: Polity Press.

Blake, William (1970 [1789/1794]) *Songs of Innocence and Experience*. Oxford: Oxford University Press.

Borges, Jorge Luis (1970) 'The Fearful Sphere of Pascal', in *Labyrinths*, pp. 224–7. London: Penguin.

Buckley, Michael (1987) *At the Origins of Modern Atheism*. New Haven and London: Yale University Press.

Byrne, James M. (ed.) (1993) *The Christian Understanding of God Today*. Dublin: Columba Press.

Byrne, James M. (1997) *Religion and the Enlightenment from Descartes to Kant*. Louisville, KY: Westminster John Knox Press.

Calvin, John (2000 [1559]) *Institutes of the Christian Religion*, in Carter Lindberg (ed.), *The European Reformations Sourcebook*, pp. 173–5. Oxford: Blackwell.

Caputo, John D. and Michael J. Scanlon (eds) (1999) *God, the Gift and Postmodernism*. Bloomington and Indianapolis: Indiana University Press.

Carver, Raymond (1994 [1988]) 'A Small Good Thing', in Paula J. Carlson and Peter S. Hawkins (eds) *Listening For God: Contemporary Literature and the Life of Faith*. Minneapolis: Augsburg Fortress.

Clayton, Philip (2000) *The Problem of God in Modern Thought*. Grand Rapids and Cambridge: Eerdmans.

Crossan, John Dominic (1994) *The Essential Jesus: Original Sayings and Earliest Images*. Edison, NJ: Castle Books.

Cupitt, Don (1997) *After God: The Future of Religion*. London: Orion Books.

Dalai Lama (1999) *Ethics for the New Millennium*. New York: Riverhead Books.

Daly, Mary (1986 [1973]) *Beyond God the Father: Towards a Philosophy of Women's Liberation*. London: The Women's Press.

Danielson, Dennis Richard (2000) *The Book of the Cosmos: Imagining the Universe from Heraclitus to Hawking*. Cambridge, MA: Perseus.

Davies, Oliver (1991) *Meister Eckhart: Mystical Theologian*. London: SPCK.

Delbanco, Andrew (1995) *The Death of Satan: How Americans Have Lost the Sense of Evil*. New York: Farrar, Strauss and Giroux.

Derrida, Jacques (1995) *The Gift of Death*, translated by David Wills. Chicago and London: University of Chicago Press.

Derrida, Jacques and Gianni Vattimo (eds) (1998) *Religion: Cultural Memory in the Present*. Stanford, CA: Stanford University Press.

Diamond, John (2000) 'Reasons to be Cheerful'. London: *Observer*, 31 December 2000.

Drees, Willem B. (1996) *Religion, Science and Naturalism*. Cambridge: Cambridge University Press.

Dukas, Helen and Banesh Hoffman (1979) *Albert Einstein: The Human Side*. Princeton: Princeton University Press.

Dupré, Louis (1993) *Passage to Modernity: An Essay in the Hermeneutics of Nature and Culture*. New Haven: Yale University Press.

Eckhart, Meister (1981) *The Essential Sermons, Commentaries, Treatises and Defense*, translated with introduction by Edmund Colledge, O.S.A. and Bernard McGinn. Mahwah, NJ: Paulist Press.

Eckhart, Meister (1994) *Selected Writings*, translated and edited with introduction by Oliver Davies. London: Penguin.

Ehrlich, Paul R. (2000) *Human Natures: Genes, Cultures and the Human Prospect*. Washington DC and Covedo CA: Island Press/Shearwater Books.

Einstein, Albert (1935) *The World as I See It*. London: John Lane/The Bodley Head.

Eliade, Mircea (1978) *A History of Religious Ideas, Vol. 1: From the Stone Age to the Eleusian Mysteries*, translated by Willard R. Task. Chicago: University of Chicago Press.

Fiorenza, Francis Schüssler and Gordon D. Kaufman (1998) 'God', in *Critical Terms in Religious Studies*, Mark C. Taylor (ed.). Chicago and London: University of Chicago Press) pp. 136–59.

Friedman, Richard Elliot (1995) *The Hidden Face of God*. San Francisco: Harper San Francisco.

Gingrich, Owen (2000) 'Do the Heavens Declare?' in Danielson, *The Book of the Cosmos*, pp. 522–8.

Girard, René (1977) *Violence and the Sacred*. Baltimore: Johns Hopkins University Press.

Girard, René (1987) *Things Hidden Since the Foundation of the World*. Stanford and London: Stanford University Press and Athlone Press.

Girard, René (1996) *The Girard Reader*, edited by James G. Williams. New York: Crossroad.

Goodenough, Ursula (1998) *The Sacred Depths of Nature*. Oxford: Oxford University Press.

Gregory of Nyssa (1999) 'On The Life of Moses', in *The Early Church Fathers: Gregory of Nyssa*, translated with introduction and epilogue by Anthony Meredith, SJ. London and New York: Routledge.

Guth, Alan H. (1997) *The Inflationary Universe: The Quest for a New Theory of Cosmic Origins*. Reading, MA: Helix Books.

Hadot, Pierre (1995) *Philosophy as a Way of Life: Spiritual Exercises from Socrates to Foucault*, translated by Michael Chase. Oxford: Blackwell.

Hartshorne, Charles and William L. Reese (eds) (2000) *Philosophers Speak of God*. New York: Humanity Books.

Harvey, Van A. (1996 [1966]) *The Historian and the Believer: The Morality of Historical Knowledge and Christian Belief*. Urbana and Chicago: University of Illinois Press.

Heidegger, Martin (1962 [1927]) *Being and Time*, translated by John Macquarrie and Edward Robinson. Oxford: Blackwell.

Hick, John (1989) *An Interpretation of Religion: Human Responses to the Transcendent*. London: Macmillan.

Hick, John (1999) *The Fifth Dimension: An Exploration of the Spiritual Realm*. Oxford: Oneworld.

Hobbes, Thomas (n.d. [1651]) *Leviathan*, M. Oakeshott (ed.). Oxford: Blackwell.

Hume, David (1990 [1779]) *Dialogues Concerning Natural Religion*. London: Penguin Books.

Humphrey, Nicholas (1996) *Leaps of Faith: Science, Miracles and the Search for the Supernatural*. New York: Copernicus/Springer-Verlag.

Kant, Immanuel (1933 [1787]) *Critique of Pure Reason*, translated by Norman Kemp Smith. London: Macmillan.

Kant, Immanuel (1960 [1793]) *Religion Within the Limits of Reason Alone*. New York: Harper & Row.

Kaufman, Gordon D. (1996) *God, Mystery, Diversity: Christian Theology in a Pluralistic World*. Minneapolis: Fortress Press.

Kierkegaard, Søren (1946) *A Kierkegaard Anthology*, Robert Bretall (ed.). Princeton: Princeton University Press.

Kierkegaard, Søren (1960) *The Diary of Søren Kierkegaard*, Peter Rhode (ed.). New York: Citadel Press.

Knight, Margaret, and Herrick, James (eds) (1995) *Humanist Anthology: From Confucius to Attenborough*. New York: Prometheus Books.

Kolakowski, Leszek (1990) *Modernity on Endless Trial*. Chicago: University of Chicago Press.

Kolakowski, Leszek (1993) *Religion: If There is No God*, 2nd edition. London: Collins/Fontana.

Kolakowski, Leszek (1999) *Freedom, Fame, Lying and Betrayal: Essays on Everyday Life*. London: Penguin.

Küng, Hans (1978) *Does God Exist?: An Answer for Today*, translated by

Edward Quinn. London: SCM Press.

Leslie, John (1989) *Universes.* London: Routledge.

McFague, Sallie (1987) *Models of God: Theology for an Ecological, Nuclear Age.* Philadelphia: Fortress Press.

MacMullen, Ramsay and Eugene N. Lane (eds) (1992) *Paganism and Christianity, 100–425 CE: A Sourcebook.* Minneapolis: Fortress Press.

MacMullen, Ramsay (1997) *Christianity and Paganism in the Fourth to Eight Centuries.* New Haven and London: Yale University Press.

Marion, Jean-Luc (1991) *God Without Being.* Chicago and London: Chicago University Press.

Marx, Karl (1989 [1845]) 'Theses on Feuerbach', in *Selected Works.* Moscow: Progress Publishers.

Miles, Jack (1995) *God: A Biography.* New York: Vintage Books.

Nicholas of Cusa (1997) *Selected Spiritual Writings,* translated and introduced by H. Lawrence Bond. New York/Mahwah NJ: Paulist Press.

Nicholls, David (1989) *Deity and Domination: Images of God and the State in the Nineteenth and Twentieth Centuries.* London and New York: Routledge.

Nietzsche, Friedrich (1987) *A Nietzsche Reader,* selected and translated by A. J. Hollingdale. London: Penguin.

Panikkar, Raimon (1997) 'Nine Ways Not to Talk about God', *Cross Currents,* Vol. 47 No. 2, pp. 149–53.

Pascal, Blaise (1966 [1670]) *Pensées,* translated by A. J. Krailsheimer. London: Penguin.

Pelikan, Jaroslav (1993) *Christianity and Classical Culture: The Metamorphosis of Natural Theology in the Christian Encounter with Hellenism.* New Haven and London: Yale University Press.

Price, Reynolds (1999) *Letter to A Man in the Fire: Does God Exist and Does He Care?* New York: Scribner.

Pseudo-Dionysius (1987) *The Divine Names* and *The Mystical Theology* in *Pseudo-Dionysius: The Complete Works,* translated by Colm Lubheid. New York and Mahwah: Paulist Press.

Rubenstein, Richard E. (1999) *When Jesus Became God: The Struggle to Define Christianity During the Last Days of Rome.* San Diego, New York, London: Harcourt.

Sartre, Jean-Paul (1980) *Existentialism and Humanism,* translated with introduction by Philip Mairet. London: Methuen.

Schleiermacher, Friedrich (1988 [1799]) *On Religion: Speeches to its Cultured Despisers,* translated with introduction and notes by

Richard Crouter. Cambridge: Cambridge University Press.

Schwartz, Regina M. (1997) *The Curse of Cain: The Violent Legacy of Monotheism*. Chicago and London: University of Chicago Press.

Scruton, Roger (1996) *An Intelligent Person's Guide to Philosophy*. London: Duckworth.

Searle, John (1999) *Mind, Language and Society: Philosophy in the Real World*. London: Weidenfeld and Nicolson.

Shermer, Michael (2000) *How We Believe: The Search for God in an Age of Science*. New York: W. H. Freeman and Company.

Smolin, Lee (1997) *The Life of the Cosmos*. New York: Oxford University Press.

Spong, John Shelby (1998) *Why Christianity Must Change or Die*. San Francisco: Harper.

Stannard, Russell (2000) *The God Experiment: Can Science Prove the Existence of God?* Mahwah, NJ: Hidden Spring/Paulist Press.

Tattersall, Ian (1998) *Becoming Human: Evolution and Human Uniqueness*. Oxford: Oxford University Press.

Tillich, Paul (1984 [1951]) *Systematic Theology,* Vol. 1. London: SCM Press.

Tillich, Paul (1979 [1952]) *The Courage to Be*. London: Collins.

Turner, Denys (1995) *The Darkness of God: Negativity in Christian Mysticism*. Cambridge: Cambridge University Press.

Vattimo, Gianni (1999) *Belief*. London: Polity Press.

Ward, Keith (1996) *God, Chance and Necessity*. Oxford: Oneworld.

Ward, Keith (1998) *God, Faith and the New Millennium: Christian Belief in an Age of Science*. Oxford: Oneworld.

Weinberg, Steven (1977) *The First Three Minutes: A Modern View of the Origin of the Universe*. New York: Basic Books.

Weinberg, Steven (1999) 'A Designer Universe?', *The New York Review of Books,* Vol. XLVI No. 16, pp. 46–8.

Wilken, Robert L. (1984) *The Christians as the Romans Saw Them*. New Haven and London: Yale University Press.

Wilson, A. N. (1999) *God's Funeral*. London: John Murray.

Index